U.S. Trade and Investment Policy

Judge Lynn N. Hughes

COUNCIL *on*
FOREIGN
RELATIONS

Independent Task Force Report No. 67

Andrew H. Card and
Thomas A. Daschle, *Chairs*
Edward Alden and
Matthew J. Slaughter, *Project Directors*

U.S. Trade and Investment Policy

The Council on Foreign Relations (CFR) is an independent, nonpartisan membership organization, think tank, and publisher dedicated to being a resource for its members, government officials, business executives, journalists, educators and students, civic and religious leaders, and other interested citizens in order to help them better understand the world and the foreign policy choices facing the United States and other countries. Founded in 1921, CFR carries out its mission by maintaining a diverse membership, with special programs to promote interest and develop expertise in the next generation of foreign policy leaders; convening meetings at its headquarters in New York and in Washington, DC, and other cities where senior government officials, members of Congress, global leaders, and prominent thinkers come together with CFR members to discuss and debate major international issues; supporting a Studies Program that fosters independent research, enabling CFR scholars to produce articles, reports, and books and hold roundtables that analyze foreign policy issues and make concrete policy recommendations; publishing *Foreign Affairs*, the preeminent journal on international affairs and U.S. foreign policy; sponsoring Independent Task Forces that produce reports with both findings and policy prescriptions on the most important foreign policy topics; and providing up-to-date information and analysis about world events and American foreign policy on its website, www.cfr.org.

The Council on Foreign Relations takes no institutional positions on policy issues and has no affiliation with the U.S. government. All views expressed in its publications and on its website are the sole responsibility of the author or authors.

The Council on Foreign Relations sponsors Independent Task Forces to assess issues of current and critical importance to U.S. foreign policy and provide policymakers with concrete judgments and recommendations. Diverse in backgrounds and perspectives, Task Force members aim to reach a meaningful consensus on policy through private and nonpartisan deliberations. Once launched, Task Forces are independent of CFR and solely responsible for the content of their reports. Task Force members are asked to join a consensus signifying that they endorse "the general policy thrust and judgments reached by the group, though not necessarily every finding and recommendation." Each Task Force member also has the option of putting forward an additional or dissenting view. Members' affiliations are listed for identification purposes only and do not imply institutional endorsement. Task Force observers participate in discussions, but are not asked to join the consensus.

For further information about CFR or this Task Force, please write to the Council on Foreign Relations, 58 East 68th Street, New York, NY 10065, or call the Communications office at 212.434.9888. Visit CFR's website at www.cfr.org.

This report is printed on paper that is FSC® certified by Rainforest Alliance, which promotes environmentally responsible, socially beneficial, and economically viable management of the world's forests.

MIX
Paper from
responsible sources
FSC® C015782

Task Force Members

Task Force members are asked to join a consensus signifying that they endorse "the general policy thrust and judgments reached by the group, though not necessarily every finding and recommendation." They participate in the Task Force in their individual, not institutional, capacities.

Edward Alden
Council on Foreign Relations

Nancy Birdsall*
Center for Global Development

James J. Blanchard
DLA Piper LLP

Andrew H. Card
*Bush School of Government
and Public Service,
Texas A&M University*

Thomas A. Daschle
DLA Piper LLP

I. M. (Mac) Destler
*University of Maryland;
Peterson Institute for
International Economics*

Harold E. Ford Jr.
*Morgan Stanley;
New York University*

Leo W. Gerard†
United Steelworkers

Daniel R. Glickman
*Aspen Institute Congressional
Program; Bipartisan Policy Center*

Robert E. Litan
*Ewing Marion Kauffman
Foundation; Brookings Institution*

Trent Lott*
Patton Boggs LLP

Kevin G. Nealer
The Scowcroft Group

James W. Owens*
Caterpillar Inc.

William F. Owens
University of Denver

Pamela S. Passman
Microsoft Corporation

*The individual has endorsed the report and signed an additional or dissenting view.

†Gerard participated as a member of the Task Force but did not endorse the general thrust of the final report. He submitted a dissenting view.

Contents

Foreword

Ten years have passed since the Council on Foreign Relations (CFR) last convened an Independent Task Force to address U.S. trade policy. Over the course of the decade, as Americans witnessed dramatic turns of global economic fortune and stagnant or declining wages and benefits at home, their traditional wariness of international trade has cooled to near antipathy.

This trend is a cause for real concern, because global trade has in fact brought enormous economic benefit to the United States and the rest of the world. In the coming decades, the booming markets in Asia, Latin America, and Africa will be among the world's most important economic engines, and exporting to them will be crucial to creating the high-wage jobs America needs.

Moreover, trade has been and remains a major strategic instrument of American foreign policy. It binds together countries in a broad and deep economic network that constitutes a bulwark against conflict; it is also a fundamental mechanism of development that contributes to growth and works against state failure.

The report of this bipartisan Independent Task Force calls on the U.S. administration and Congress to adopt trade and investment policies that maximize the benefits to the American people and U.S. foreign policy from global economic engagement.

The trade agenda outlined in this report stands on seven pillars: an ambitious trade negotiation strategy to open markets for the most competitive U.S. sectors, especially within emerging markets; the implementation of a National Investment Initiative to coordinate investment policy and attract good jobs to the United States; a renewed effort to bolster trade enforcement; increased government promotion of American exports; the expansion of trade to foster development in the world's poorest countries; comprehensive worker adjustment and retraining programs; and the establishment of a presidential mandate to negotiate trade-opening agreements with an assurance of timely congressional action. The Task Force recommends that the administration start by pushing harder for ratification of the three free trade agreements—with South Korea, Colombia, and Panama—still awaiting passage in the Congress.

This independent study is one of several projects undertaken by CFR to commemorate its ninetieth year through an initiative focused on "Renewing America." Through its history, CFR has largely focused on the classic questions of foreign policy, but issues of traditionally domestic concern—such as trade policies, debt, education, immigration, and infrastructure—will increasingly represent the principal set of challenges to U.S. power and leadership abroad.

I would like to thank the Task Force chairs, Andrew H. Card and Thomas A. Daschle, for their many contributions to this project. My thanks extend to all of the distinguished Task Force members for lending their time, knowledge, and considerable experience to produce a thoughtful report.

I invite readers also to review the additional and dissenting views written by several Task Force members that appear at the end of the report. The report of an Independent Task Force is a document that represents consensus among the group, and each signatory endorses the broad thrust of the policy recommendations. However, these additional views provide valuable insight into the breadth of the debate and demonstrate the complexity of the issues at hand.

Finally, this report would not be possible without the supervision of Anya Schmemann, CFR's Task Force Program director, who ably guided this project from beginning to end, as well as CFR's Senior Fellows Edward Alden and Matthew J. Slaughter, who skillfully directed the Task Force and coauthored this report.

Richard N. Haass
President
Council on Foreign Relations
September 2011

Acknowledgments

Some months before Richard Haass asked us to serve as co-project directors for this Task Force, we sat down together over a long dinner in Washington, DC, and shared our concerns over the direction of the U.S. economy in the face of rising global competition. As fathers of teenage or soon-to-be-teenage children, we voiced worries that the United States was losing its ability to create the sort of well-paying jobs that had been abundant in this country for many generations. In particular, we talked about how international trade and investment, which in the past had helped to deliver rising prosperity, no longer seemed to be generating the same gains for too many Americans.

The report of the Independent Task Force on U.S. Trade and Investment Policy is the product of a tremendous effort by a distinguished group of Task Force members to address the question of that dinner: how trade can do more for more Americans. We greatly appreciate the time, attention, and expertise these members devoted to this project. In particular, we thank our distinguished chairs, Andrew H. Card and Thomas A. Daschle, who brought a lifetime of experience, wisdom, and leadership to bear in building common ground on an issue where divisions have grown sharper in recent decades. It has been a privilege to work with both of them.

We are thankful to several people who met with and briefed the Task Force group, including U.S. secretary of the treasury Timothy F. Geithner and former U.S. trade representatives Charlene Barshefsky, Carla A. Hills, Mickey Kantor, and Susan Schwab.

We also received helpful input from CFR members, many of whom have extraordinary expertise on trade issues. The DC Meetings team organized an event with CFR members in Washington, led by Task Force members John K. Veroneau and Alan W. Wolff; and the NY Meetings team organized an event for CFR members in New York. The National Program team arranged a series of sessions with CFR members in California and Florida, led by John Yochelson, Joseph K. Hurd III, and

Charles E. Cobb Jr. The Term Member Program sponsored a meeting in Washington, DC, led by Mitul Desai, and the Washington Program organized a meeting with foreign ambassadors and other embassy officials, led by Task Force member Nancy Birdsall and moderated by Chris Tuttle. These sessions were extremely valuable in shaping the report.

We also benefited from the insights shared at two dinner meetings that brought together members of Congress, senior officials of the administration, and the trade community. These events were led by Madeleine K. Albright, Kenneth M. Duberstein, Richard A. Gephardt, and Vin Weber and organized by Kay King.

Edward Alden would also like to thank Shanker Singham, Jennifer Harris, Mark Anderson, and Jutta Hennig for their valuable suggestions, as well as the participants in the CFR Roundtable Series on U.S. Competitiveness.

Matthew Slaughter would also like to thank coauthors and colleagues who have helped shape ideas: Paul Danos, Gordon Hanson, Jonathan Haskel, Robert Lawrence, Edward Leamer, Ken Scheve, Mara Tchalakov, and David Wessel.

We are grateful to many at CFR: CFR's Publications team assisted in editing the report and readied it for publication. CFR's Communications, Corporate, External Affairs, and Outreach teams all worked to ensure that the report reaches the widest audience possible.

Anya Schmemann and Kristin Lewis of CFR's Task Force Program, and our research associate Kate Pynoos, were instrumental to this project from beginning to end, from the selection of Task Force members to the convening of meetings to the careful editing of multiple drafts. We are indebted to them for their assistance and for keeping the project on track.

We are grateful to CFR President Richard N. Haass and Director of Studies James M. Lindsay for giving us the opportunity to direct this effort. We also thank Google, Inc., for generously supporting this project, and Bernard L. Schwartz for his ongoing generous support of CFR's work on American competitiveness.

While this report is the product of the Task Force, we take responsibility for its content and note that any omissions or mistakes are ours. Once again, our sincere thanks to all who contributed to this effort.

Edward Alden
Matthew J. Slaughter
Project Directors

Acronyms

AD/CVD	antidumping/countervailing duty
AGOA	African Growth and Opportunity Act
APEC	Asia-Pacific Economic Cooperation
ASEAN	Association of Southeast Asian Nations
ATPA	Andean Trade Preference Act
BEA	Bureau of Economic Analysis
BIT	bilateral investment treaty
BRIC	Brazil, Russia, India, and China
CAFTA	Central American Free Trade Agreement
CBI	Caribbean Basin Initiative
CFIUS	Committee on Foreign Investment in the United States
CNOOC	China National Offshore Oil Corporation
EC	European Commission
ECA	Export Credit Agency
EPA	Economic Partnership Agreement
EU	European Union
FDI	foreign direct investment
FTA	free trade agreement
FTAA	Free Trade Area of the Americas
G20	Group of 20
GATT	General Agreement on Tariffs and Trade
GDP	gross domestic product
GPA	Government Procurement Agreement
GSP	Generalized System of Preferences

IMF	International Monetary Fund
IP	intellectual property
IPR	intellectual property rights
IRS	Internal Revenue Service
IT	information technology
ITA	Information Technology Agreement
ITC	International Trade Commission
JCCT	Joint Commission on Cooperation and Trade
M&A	mergers and acquisitions
MNC	multinational companies
NAFTA	North American Free Trade Agreement
NEI	National Export Initiative
NII	National Investment Initiative
NTE	National Trade Estimate
OECD	Organization for Economic Cooperation and Development
R&D	research and development
SED	Strategic and Economic Dialogue
SOE	state-owned enterprises
SPP	Security and Prosperity Partnership
TAA	Trade Adjustment Assistance
TIFA	Trade and Investment Framework Agreement
TPA	Trade Promotion Authority
TPP	Trans-Pacific Partnership
UI	unemployment insurance
UNSD	United Nations Statistics Division
USTR	United States Trade Representative
VAT	value-added tax
VER	voluntary export restraint
WIA	Workforce Investment Act
WTO	World Trade Organization

Task Force Report

Executive Summary

The growth of global trade and investment has brought significant benefits to the United States and to the rest of the world. Freer trade and investment, facilitated by rules the United States led in negotiating and implementing, have alleviated poverty, raised average standards of living, and discouraged conflict.

But over the past two decades, American support for trade liberalization has waned. Today, the United States lacks an ambitious trade policy and has not kept pace with other countries in opening new markets abroad, especially in the fast-growing economies of Asia and Latin America that are now major engines of global growth.

If the United States is to prosper in today's global economy, it must enhance its ability to attract the investment and jobs linked to producing goods and services for these large and prospering markets. In short, the United States must become a great trading nation.

The primary reason for the stalling of U.S. trade policy is the serious employment and income pressures so many Americans face. Americans recognize the benefits of trade in terms of lower-priced and higher-quality consumer products and acknowledge the benefits for poorer countries trading with the United States. But these gains have not been enough to maintain public support for further trade opening.

Americans have understandably become more wary of international competition, both because wages over the past decade have stagnated for almost all Americans and because the Great Recession destroyed millions of jobs. This wariness accords with evidence that at least some of these wage pressures stem from trade and other globalization forces. There are challenges on many fronts—including education, infrastructure, government debts, regulation, and immigration policies—but U.S. trade and investment strategies are a critical part of the equation.

Even with the recent strong growth in exports, the United States remains an export underperformer. Its share of worldwide foreign direct investment has also fallen sharply compared with other advanced economies. Creation of high-wage U.S. jobs by multinational companies, after a strong decade in the 1990s, has stalled, and these companies have shed nearly three million jobs over the past decade.

Unless the U.S. government can devise and implement trade and investment policies that benefit more Americans by sparking greater investment and jobs in the United States linked to the global economy, it will be impossible to rebuild public support for trade policy.

This report calls for the administration and Congress to adopt a pro-America trade policy that brings to more Americans more of the benefits of global engagement, within the framework of a strengthened, rules-based trading system.

The Task Force recommends a new trade and investment strategy based on seven pillars:

- An ambitious trade-negotiations agenda that opens markets for the most competitive U.S.-produced goods and services, especially the biggest and fastest-growing emerging markets
- A National Investment Initiative that would coordinate policies on inward and outbound investment to encourage the location in the United States of high-wage, high-productivity jobs
- A robust and strategic trade enforcement effort, with the U.S. government playing a more proactive role in ensuring that U.S. companies and workers are not harmed by trade agreement violations
- Greater efforts to promote exports through more competitive export financing and a more active government role in supporting U.S. overseas sales
- Expanded use of trade to foster development in the world's poorest countries
- A comprehensive worker adjustment and retraining policy
- A new deal with Congress to give the president a mandate to negotiate trade-opening agreements with an assurance of timely congressional action

The Task Force believes strongly that Americans, and both parties in Congress, can support such an approach. The report lays out a strategy to enable the United States to engage more successfully in international markets in a way that brings the benefits of trade and investment to more Americans.

The United States still has many economic strengths, and a new set of trade and investment policies built on those strengths will pay enormous dividends.

Introduction

The expansion of global trade in the past half century is one of the signature accomplishments of modern U.S. foreign policy. Out of the wreckage of the Great Depression and World War II, American leaders and their allies in Europe, Japan, Canada, and elsewhere established international rules for commerce that allowed for an unprecedented growth in the exchange of goods and services across borders.

The benefits have been substantial. Economic growth fueled in part by integration into the world economy has helped lift hundreds of millions of people out of poverty, the highest rate of poverty reduction in human history. Peaceful exchange has helped reduce conflict by offering countries new ways to enrich themselves without territorial conquest. And the structure of international rules built to resolve trade and investment disputes has helped contain protectionist responses, even in the face of the worst global economic downturn since the Great Depression.

The United States has gained in numerous ways. Liberalization of trade and investment over the past half century has made Americans wealthier than they could have become in a closed economy. Opening the U.S. market to imported goods has strengthened U.S. foreign policy by improving living standards in allied countries in Europe, Asia, and Latin America. It has fostered deep engagement with many countries in which the United States has strategic interests but no military presence. And it has promoted core U.S. beliefs about how societies are best structured to benefit their citizens, including free enterprise, democratic governance, open markets, respect for workers' rights and the environment, and transparent regulation.

Yet Americans today are deeply ambivalent about the value of continued trade opening and unsure whether the country should remain at the forefront of trade liberalization. Although the benefits of an active trade policy are well understood, opening of trade in recent years has not done enough to deliver broad-based job and income growth to Americans.

Americans as consumers have enjoyed lower prices and higher quality from imports. U.S. companies have improved efficiency and raised productivity in response to international competition. But most Americans over the past decade have not seen wage gains, more have been unemployed and for longer periods, and income inequality has been increasing faster than in most other countries. As a consequence, Americans are more skeptical about the benefits of trade than citizens in virtually any other country.[1] Even before the financial crisis and the recession, Americans had come to see trade as more of a threat to their well-being than as an opportunity for economic growth, a reversal of the optimism that existed in the 1990s.[2]

Congress too has been split, lawmakers either refusing to approve additional trade-opening agreements or passing such deals by the narrowest of majorities. As a result, the U.S. government has been unable to carry out an ambitious trade and investment policy that responds to the rapid changes taking place in the global economy. For too long the United States has been on the sidelines as other countries have found new ways to deepen their commercial relationships. U.S. trade policy lacks both direction and momentum at a time when Americans are facing the most pressing economic challenges in generations.

This stalemate has already harmed U.S. interests and will do more if it remains unresolved. The world is in the midst of a historic transition that has been called the great convergence, in which many developing economies are growing at rates that are propelling hundreds of millions of people into Western, middle-class standards of living. Most of the world's economic growth is now taking place in these countries—not in the older, advanced economies of Europe, North America, and Japan. In the five years from 2005 to the first quarter of 2010, output in emerging economies rose by 41 percent (including 70 percent in China and 55 percent in India), but in advanced economies by only 5 percent.[3] Even as emerging countries are producing and exporting more, their demand for goods and services from advanced economies is exploding, creating enormous opportunities for the increased mutual benefits that trade offers.

Yet the United States is not nearly as well placed as it should be to take advantage of these opportunities. Other countries have been pursuing more aggressive trade strategies to open markets for their goods and services and have made greater efforts to attract job-creating foreign investment. The United States, for all its economic success, has never been a great trading nation. A large domestic market long allowed this country to prosper with limited access to foreign markets. As recently as 1970, trade was just 10 percent of the total U.S. gross domestic product (GDP); today, although more than 25 percent, it is the lowest among any developed economy other than Japan.

The future prosperity of the United States will require it to become a thriving trading nation. U.S. economic growth increasingly depends on the United States being a location for enterprises that sell to global markets. Yet U.S. export growth has been relatively weak. Even with the encouraging export surge over the past year, the U.S. share of global exports declined between 2000 and 2011 compared with most other advanced economies (see Figure 1).

Export-related jobs tend to pay more than those that produce goods or services for the domestic market, but export growth has not been strong enough to spread those benefits widely to Americans.[4] In 2009, exports accounted directly for about 8.5 million jobs, roughly the same as in 1999. Even before the recession, the number of export jobs was just over 10 million, less than 7 percent of total U.S. employment, a figure that has not changed significantly in nearly two decades despite the tremendous growth in overseas markets.[5] Over the past two decades, nearly all job growth in the U.S. economy has been in nontradable sectors, particularly health care and government.[6] Given much tighter government budgets for the foreseeable future, U.S. employment growth will require a much stronger performance in the tradable sectors (see Figure 2).[7]

Nor has U.S. foreign direct investment (FDI), another important source of job creation and innovation, kept pace with that of other advanced economies. Although the U.S. share of global FDI stock rose sharply in the 1990s—and the United States remains the most attractive investment location in the world—that share has fallen sharply over the past decade (see Figure 3).

In a world where most trade takes place among different parts of multinational companies, the United States must become more adept at exploiting its advantages in the global supply chain. For instance, the U.S. business environment has long encouraged innovation in the production of goods, the delivery of services, and the logistics of international commerce. Washington should be actively involved in shaping

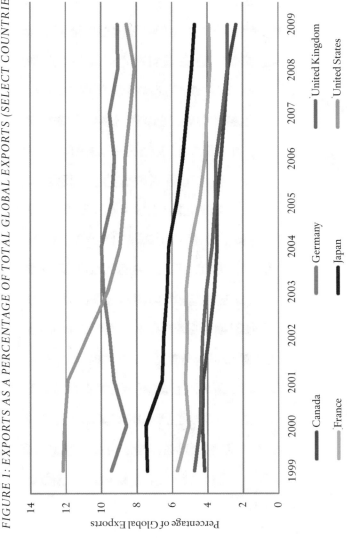

FIGURE 1: EXPORTS AS A PERCENTAGE OF TOTAL GLOBAL EXPORTS (SELECT COUNTRIES)

Percentage of Global Exports

14
12
10
8
6
4
2
0

1999   2000   2001   2002   2003   2004   2005   2006   2007   2008   2009

Canada   Germany   United Kingdom
France   Japan   United States

Source: IMF Direction of Trade Statistics

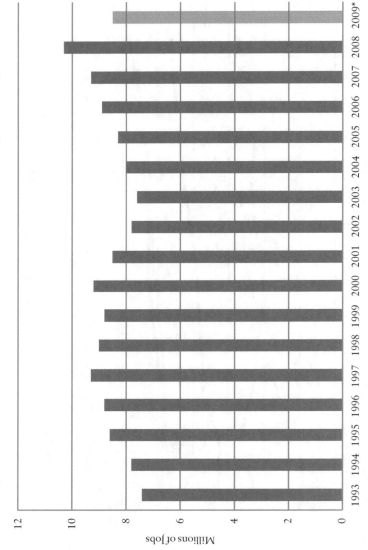

FIGURE 2: JOBS SUPPORTED BY EXPORTS OF GOODS AND SERVICES (1993–2009)

Source: Estimates compiled by U.S. Department of Commerce, Office of the Chief Economist. Note: 2009 is a preliminary estimate.

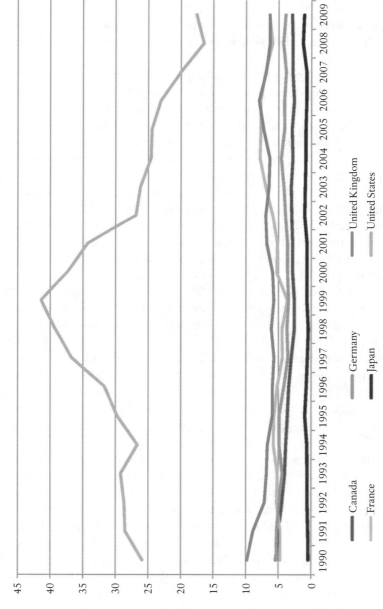

FIGURE 3: FDI STOCK IN SELECT ECONOMIES AS PERCENTAGE OF TOTAL WORLD STOCK

Canada
France
Germany
Japan
United Kingdom
United States

Source: UNCTADStat 2010

and enforcing trade rules that play to U.S. strengths and ensure that those advantages are not undermined by foreign government subsidies, technology transfer requirements, or inadequate protection of intellectual property.

The United States also cannot afford to relinquish trade policy as a diplomatic and development tool. Opening new trade opportunities fosters growth and expands economic opportunities in poorer countries, which is especially important as foreign aid budgets face further tightening. Economic engagement remains one of the best ways the United States can lead by example, to offer paths for adversaries to become friends and to encourage political transformation in closed societies. Yet the U.S. president has not had congressional negotiating authority since the Trade Promotion Authority (TPA) expired in 2007. And, in early 2011, Congress allowed two programs that eliminate tariffs on many imports from developing countries—the Generalized System of Preferences (GSP) and the Andean Trade Preference Act (ATPA)— to lapse.

The benefits of trade need to be realized by the American people, not only through cheaper and better television sets and smart phones, but also through more jobs and higher incomes. In the absence of such gains, it will be increasingly difficult for the United States to sustain its global leadership on trade, which would have negative consequences for the U.S. economy, foreign policy and national security, and global stability. The United States has not historically worried much about how to make itself an attractive location for investment geared toward exports. Given a rapidly changing global economy, this mindset needs to change.

In his 2010 State of the Union speech, U.S. president Barack Obama called for a "National Export Initiative" to double American exports in five years and to create two million jobs. "We have to seek new markets aggressively, just as our competitors are," he said. "If America sits on the sidelines while other nations sign trade deals, we will lose the chance to create jobs on our shores. But realizing those benefits also means enforcing those agreements so our trading partners play by the rules." The weaker dollar, and the global recovery from the 2008–2009 recession, contributed to strong U.S. export growth in 2010 and the first half of 2011; exports rose by 17 percent last year. But achieving the ambitious goal of doubling exports by 2015 will require, among other things, a more assertive and focused trade and investment policy that plays to

America's economic strengths in such areas as sophisticated manufactured goods, services, and agriculture.

The United States has negotiated trade agreements that have improved the operation of markets around the world through greater transparency, nondiscrimination, and respect for private investments. Such certainty is the bedrock that allows economies to grow and prosper. But the United States has not done nearly as well at bringing the economic benefits of that rules-based system to its own people.

The Task Force believes that the challenge is clear. Unless the United States develops and sustains a trade policy that yields greater benefits for Americans in job and wage growth, it will be difficult to build the political consensus needed to move forward. Policies that encourage the location of research, development, and production of tradable goods and services in the United States must be adopted.

The United States should implement a pro-America trade policy that brings to a greater number of Americans more of the benefits of economic growth around the world, within the framework of a strengthened, rules-based trading system.

Goals of U.S. Trade Policy

Through its trade policies, the United States has tried to set and enforce rules for fair competition in the global economy, not only by lowering tariff barriers, but also by improving the treatment of foreign investors, opening procurement by governments, limiting subsidies, pressing for better enforcement of labor and environmental standards, and protecting intellectual property.

Historically, international trade primarily involved the export and import of finished products. Today, most international trade takes place among separate arms of multinational companies that may divide up the production of a single finished good among many countries. What are counted as imports and exports are often components in a global supply chain that result in a finished product (see sidebar next page). Determining what constitutes an American product and what constitutes a foreign product has become impossible in some industries, particularly high-technology industries. Economic advantages may arise more from the location of research and development (R&D) and innovation capabilities than from the assembly and export of finished goods that are counted in trade statistics. A strategy to increase the benefits of trade to the United States needs to focus on maximizing the value added to goods and services by companies and employees inside the United States.

In addition, as trade has grown more important to the U.S. economy, it has become harder to distinguish between trade and other aspects of economic policy. Trade-liberalizing agreements, for instance, make it easier for U.S. goods and services to be sold abroad and for foreign goods and services to be sold in the United States. Increased competition and larger markets encourage specialization that raises productivity, reduces prices to consumers, and boosts overall wealth.

But how well the United States or any other economy responds to those opportunities is influenced by many factors other than trade

IMPROVING TRADE STATISTICS

The collection and dissemination of trade statistics have not kept pace with the changing patterns of trade that mark the current era of globalization. That lack of adequate data has made it harder for U.S. trade negotiators to set and pursue trade priorities that support U.S. interests, and has distorted the public debate over trade.

The primary area in which trade statistics should be adapted is in the measurement of trade flows. Unlike manufacturing of fifty years ago, today many traded goods are not made in a single country. Instead, companies have set up intricate global supply chains in which various stages of the production of a single product are located in several different countries. Despite this change, trade statistics still attribute the full value to the country from which the good is exported to its final consumer destination. As a consequence, bilateral trade imbalances with the destination market can be greatly inflated by trade in intermediate products, and can provide a distorted picture of bilateral trade flows. A recent study of Apple's iPhone, for instance, found that while China exported more than $2 billion worth of finished iPhones to the United States in 2009, the Chinese value added per phone was only $6.50, or just 3.6 percent of the total export value (the U.S. value added that year was $542 million).[8] Under current trade statistics, the iPhone alone contributed $1.9 billion to the U.S. trade deficit with China that year, a highly inflated figure.

One possible solution to this problem would be measuring trade flows in value-added terms, which involves attributing the share of total value of each product to the country in which that share was created or produced. Various studies have found that the U.S. bilateral trade deficit with China would be 20 to 40 percent lower if estimated in value-added terms. This reflects the fact that Chinese goods exported to the United States contain only 20 to 35 percent of domestic value added.[9]

Measuring trade flows by where value is added could also be served by a shift to firm-level analysis, which has been promoted by Pascal Lamy, director-general of the World Trade Organization (WTO).[10] Participants in a February 2011 United Nations

(continued next page)

(continued)

Statistics Division (UNSD), Eurostat, and WTO-hosted "Global Forum on Trade Statistics" encouraged all countries to develop a national register to identify enterprises active in international trade and to link those enterprise statistics to existing trade data.[11] The WTO's "Made in the World" initiative is seeking to add this new perspective to how world trade is measured.

In addition, there is significant room for improvement in how services trade data is measured. Unlike manufactured goods traded across borders, which can be counted at points of shipment, data on the services sector is collected in a variety of surveys, which often lag in their release and have gaps across industry coverage. The services sector accounts for about one third of total U.S. exports, and the U.S. trade data system needs to provide more comprehensive, disaggregated information on a variety of areas of services trade. As Francisco Sanchez, U.S. undersecretary of commerce for international trade, pointed out in September 2010, the United States does not have detailed data on, for example, "what the United States imports from and exports to Colombia in services. Nor do we know our current trade balance in health care services." Comprehensive data on specific manufactured exports can be generated in a relatively short time frame, he noted, but the United States does not disseminate similar data on exports of legal services for a year or more.[12] Detailed data on exported services are available almost exclusively from survey-based reports compiled by the Census Bureau, which include the five-year economic census data and the Services Annual Survey. The Bureau of Economic Analysis (BEA) also collects data on exports of services by type of services from surveys that it conducts and from data provided by other government agencies and private sources. The challenge is to make public the significant amount of data in the private sector, while respecting confidentiality rules and avoiding company-reporting burden.[13]

The Task Force recommends that the U.S. government undertake a major effort to improve the collection and dissemination of trade data, including supporting international initiatives currently under way in the WTO and the Organization for Economic Cooperation and Development (OECD).

policy. These include education and workforce training, availability and cost of capital, currency values, quality of infrastructure, relative tax burdens, costs and effectiveness of domestic regulation, visas and immigration policy, and investment in R&D.[14] Although trade policy is critical, it would not be at the top of this list in determining whether any nation succeeds in international competition. The best trade policy in the world may do little to improve living standards if other policies leave the country ill-equipped for increased competition. To increase higher-wage employment, the United States needs to have the best trained, most innovative and productive workforce and a set of government policies that support investment and job growth in the United States.

Trade policy must be part of a broader national effort to improve the capacity of Americans to compete in the global economy. Trade and investment policies can be discussed sensibly only in this larger context. But this should not discourage creative thinking about how trade could do more to raise U.S. living standards. Too often, proponents of liberalized trade have used the shortcomings of domestic policy to deflect any deeper discussion about the direction of U.S. trade policy. Similarly, critics of U.S. trade policies often blame trade agreements for economic problems that are largely the consequences of failings in other areas. Although the United States must improve its domestic capacity to compete in the global economy, U.S. trade and investment policies should be judged by the contribution they make to improving American living standards and advancing America's broader interests.

The Task Force believes that the primary goal of U.S. trade policy should be to establish and enforce rules for the international exchange of goods and services that bring the greatest possible benefits to the American people, while also promoting the larger foreign policy interests of the United States.

Current U.S. Policy

American trade policy has for more than seventy-five years been built on foundations Congress established in the depths of the Great Depression. In response to the damaging effects of tariff increases, the Reciprocal Trade Agreements Act of 1934 authorized the administration to reduce U.S. tariffs through negotiations with other countries that would agree to similar tariff reductions. Over time, the United States became increasingly committed to lowering barriers worldwide to the freer movement of goods, services, and investment capital. As the world's most competitive economy, it was thought, the United States—specifically, its companies and workers—would gain from larger markets, and trade expansion would help raise living standards in developing countries and strengthen U.S. Cold War alliances.

As long as certain protections against "unfair trade" were maintained or strengthened, Congress consistently endorsed these efforts. It approved the Trade Expansion Act of 1962 by an overwhelming bipartisan vote, giving President John F. Kennedy additional authority to negotiate tariff reductions and adding new ways for companies to protect themselves against surges of imports, and creating the Trade Adjustment Assistance (TAA) program to help displaced workers. In 1974, Congress approved so-called fast-track trade negotiating authority, allowing the administration to negotiate changes to trade-distorting regulations as well as tariff reductions and have these agreements voted on by Congress without amendments and within strict time limits. The 1988 Trade Act, which passed by large bipartisan majorities, combined a series of new measures to ensure tough enforcement of trading rules with authority for the administration to pursue the most ambitious trade agreements in U.S. history. The George H.W. Bush administration concluded the North American Free Trade Agreement (NAFTA) with Canada and Mexico. The Clinton administration finished the Uruguay Round of the General Agreement on Tariffs and Trade (GATT) and won congressional assent for both, adding side agreements to the NAFTA to address concerns over labor and environmental standards in Mexico.

Since NAFTA, the United States has pushed for enforceable commitments on labor and environment in each of its subsequent bilateral and regional trade agreements and has included labor commitments in its trade preference programs. The free trade agreement (FTA) with Jordan, negotiated in 2000, for the first time included the commitment to uphold national labor and environmental standards as part of the core text of the agreement, subject to the same dispute settlement procedures as commercial disputes. And the pact noted that the two countries were committed to upholding international mandatory labor standards. The U.S.-Peru FTA in 2006 went a step further by requiring the parties to "adopt and maintain" international labor standards and multilateral environmental commitments. While the link between trade, labor, and environment has remained contentious, it has become a core part of the U.S. trade agenda, alongside efforts to improve intellectual property protection, expand coverage of service industries, and open government procurement markets.[15]

Over the past two decades, however, political divisions over trade have continued to deepen. The TPA lapsed in 1994 and was not renewed until 2002, and then only after the House passed the bill by a single vote that required significant arm-twisting or special deals for a handful of recalcitrant members. It was, as I. M. Destler wrote, "the most partisan congressional vote on such a bill since the 1930s."[16] The administration of President George W. Bush launched the Doha Round of world trade negotiations and negotiated bilateral or regional trade agreements with more than a dozen countries. Some, such as the agreements with Australia and Peru, drew strong bipartisan support. But the Central American Free Trade Agreement (CAFTA) passed the House by just two votes, and Congress did not vote on the final three agreements negotiated by the Bush administration—with South Korea, Panama, and Colombia.

In the 2008 U.S. Trade Representative (USTR) Trade Policy Agenda and 2007 Annual Report presented to Congress, the Bush administration challenged opponents of its trade policies, pointing to rising productivity, growing exports, and falling unemployment through 2007: "Despite this record of sustained economic progress and prosperity, critics continue to promote the myth that trade is at the root of all economic ills. Close scrutiny of the facts, however, does not support their

assertions. . . . Moreover, to attempt to wall the United States off from
foreign competition and 'protect' U.S. workers would only serve to
cripple the U.S. economy and potentially induce a global trade war and
world economic slowdown."[17]

By the time President Obama took office, however, the world was in
the midst of a severe economic slowdown and trade volumes had col-
lapsed. Trade policy was not initially a high priority for the incoming
administration. It chose not to push immediately for congressional
ratification of free trade agreements with South Korea, Colombia, and
Panama, saying that all three would need to be modified to address outstanding concerns. In its first Trade Policy Agenda report to Congress
in 2009, the administration said it would not move quickly to launch
new trade negotiations.[18] Instead, the administration would focus
more on the adjustment challenges facing the American workforce
and on advancing labor rights and environmental standards abroad. It
also called for greater transparency and accountability in trade policy.
Ronald Kirk, the U.S. trade representative, did not deliver his first
formal testimony to the House Ways and Means Committee, which
oversees trade policy, until February 2011, reflecting the low priority
that trade has had on the administration's agenda.

Over the past year, however, the Obama administration has become
increasingly focused on the role that trade can play in encouraging U.S.
economic growth. Exports contributed nearly half of total U.S. GDP
growth in 2010. In its 2010 report to Congress, the administration
stated, "To improve American prosperity, we must match other countries in seeking new international markets aggressively."[19] Its March
2011 Trade Policy Agenda report also laid out a more ambitious negotiating agenda, particularly in Asia, and focused heavily on administration efforts to enforce existing trade commitments.

In September 2010, the administration released the National Export
Initiative (NEI), which set a target of doubling U.S. annual exports to
more than $3 trillion by the end of 2014. The major steps proposed by the
NEI include improved advocacy and trade promotion, increased export
financing, new efforts to remove barriers to U.S. exports, increased
enforcement of trade rules, and international negotiations through the
Group of Twenty (G20) and other bodies to encourage more balanced
global economic growth.[20]

The administration has been pursuing many of the initiatives laid out
in the NEI. Export financing through the U.S. Export-Import (Ex-Im)

Bank hit a record $24.5 billion in 2010. The administration has initiated a major overhaul of U.S. export control rules to facilitate the overseas sale of more sophisticated goods. It has worked through the G20 and in bilateral negotiations to address the issue of global imbalances, though the U.S. Treasury has resisted formally identifying China or any other country as a "currency manipulator." And the number of trade enforcement actions has increased, especially against China, continuing a trend that began at the end of the George W. Bush administration.

The Obama administration has become increasingly engaged in trade negotiations. In December 2009, it announced that it would continue a Bush negotiating initiative in Asia, the Trans-Pacific Partnership (TPP). The TPP was originally launched by four countries—New Zealand, Chile, Singapore, and Brunei—and the United States entered negotiations with them in 2008, simultaneously with Vietnam, Australia, and Peru. After a review, the administration announced that the United States would expand the negotiations "with the objective of shaping a high-standard, broad-based regional pact." In November 2011, the United States will host the summit of the Asia-Pacific Economic Cooperation (APEC) in Hawaii, which the administration hopes will give impetus to the TPP negotiations.

In December 2010, the administration announced that it had agreed with South Korea on several modifications to an FTA, commonly referred to as KORUS FTA, which was first concluded in 2007. The major changes were in the automotive sector, where South Korea has enjoyed a large trade surplus with the United States. In April, the administration announced that it had reached a new understanding with Colombia on a framework for improvement of labor rights and that it had also resolved outstanding issues with Panama, setting the stage for congressional action on the three outstanding trade agreements. As of this writing, the three agreements appeared likely to be taken up for approval by Congress following the 2011 summer recess, and were expected to proceed along with the reauthorization of the lapsed TAA program for displaced workers.

Trade, the U.S. Economy, and Public Opinion

The freer flow of trade and investment across the world has generated, and has the potential to continue generating, large gains for the United States overall, if combined with other policies supporting U.S. competitiveness. American productivity and average standards of living are higher because of globalization. Globalization allows pools of savings (whether by private households, by companies, or by governments) to be matched with investment opportunities not just at home but abroad as well; this better matching tends to boost rates of economic growth. Globalization facilitates the flow of ideas across borders, through immigration and communications technology, and within multinational companies; more and better ideas in turn tend to boost economic growth. Globalization also allows each country to concentrate its scarce resources of people and ideas in those activities with which it is well suited compared with the rest of the world. It can then export these goods and services for imports of other products that can be enjoyed in greater variety and at lower prices.

Academic studies indicate that annual U.S. national income today is at least ten percentage points of GDP ($1 trillion) higher than it would have been absent decades of trade, investment, and immigration liberalization. Looking ahead, some studies forecast that annual U.S. income could be upward of $500 billion higher with substantial liberalization of global trade and investment in both merchandise and services.[21]

But trade gains come with costs. Some communities lose companies and the jobs they support; employees may face long periods of unemployment, or only find new jobs at lower wages. The last time the Council on Foreign Relations convened a Task Force to examine U.S. trade policy, in early 2001, it was easier to argue that the benefits of trade clearly outweighed the costs. Then, the U.S. economy had near record-low levels of unemployment, and the second half of the 1990s had brought strong real-income gains for nearly all skill groups. The report, chaired by former Treasury secretary Robert E. Rubin and former White House chief of staff Kenneth M. Duberstein, and directed by the current Treasury secretary, Timothy F. Geithner, concluded accurately that "the gains from trade are broadly shared. . . . Throughout the last decade, as the United States has become significantly more open, U.S. employment and wages have increased."[22]

Today the scenario is far more challenging. Over the past ten years, nearly all American workers have experienced falling, not rising, real earnings. And in the wake of the Great Recession, there are several million fewer U.S. jobs today than a decade ago.

Trade is only a part of this equation, but it cannot be dismissed as irrelevant. Indeed, given that many broad measures of trade have intensified over the past decade—for example, the surge of traded goods flowing in and out of China, and the spreading tradability of services thanks to ongoing information technology (IT) innovations—trade and globalization have certainly factored into recent U.S. labor-market conditions.

The bottom line is that many American workers today feel anxious about their economic prospects. Their concerns are real, widespread, and legitimate. Public support for engagement with the world economy is strongly linked to personal labor-market performance. In recent years, U.S. public support for trade has dropped dramatically, and this reflects a public increasingly skeptical about whether globalization benefits them.

THE DISTRIBUTIONAL CHALLENGE: POOR LABOR-MARKET PERFORMANCE IN RECENT YEARS

The U.S. economy currently faces several deep challenges. First, U.S. companies of all sizes have yet to resume vigorous job creation. In the last recession, the United States lost 8.83 million private-sector payroll jobs—a remarkable 7.64 percent of total employment. The U.S. economy currently has about 109 million private-sector payroll jobs and 11.7 million manufacturing payroll jobs. The last times it had that few were June 1999 and April 1941, respectively. In 2010, the U.S. nonfarm business sector created an average of 101,250 payroll jobs per month. This did not even accommodate population growth, let alone refill the jobs hole in the United States.

Second, wage earnings for most Americans have been weak for many years. Recently released Internal Revenue Service (IRS) data show that in 2008 the top 1 percent of tax filers (those reporting at least $368,238 in income that year) earned 21 percent of all gross personal income, down from 23.5 percent the previous year. Income inequality has increased for the past thirty years—from just 7.9 percent of income to the top 1 percent of the population in 1977—and nearly equals the record concentrations of the late 1920s. More troubling, U.S. inequality is widening largely because of falling real incomes for all but the most skilled, highest earners.

From 2000 through 2009, only workers with a doctorate or a professional postgraduate degree—just 3.6 percent of the labor force—enjoyed increases in their average real-money incomes. All other educational cohorts, including college graduates and those with non-professional master's degrees, saw declines. What is especially new since 2000 is the falling real earnings of many high-skilled workers. In the previous generation, these groups had experienced consistently strong growth in their real and relative earnings. This trend is reflected in family earnings. In 2009, the median American household income was $49,777, barely above what it was in 1997.

TABLE 1: CHANGE IN AVERAGE EARNINGS
BY EDUCATIONAL COHORT, 2000–2009

Educational Group	U.S. Employment Share	Earnings Change
No high school degree	8.70%	–10.00%
High school diploma	28.80%	–9.40%
Some college	27.50%	–6.60%
Four-year college degree	22.50%	–5.50%
Nonprofessional master's degree	8.90%	–1.30%
Doctoral degree	1.80%	1.80%
Doctors, lawyers, and MBAs	1.80%	11.10%

Source: U.S. Census Bureau

The overall picture is sobering. Today there are fewer private-sector jobs than a decade ago, and the real earnings of nearly all these jobs are less than a decade ago. Over the twentieth century, except for the Great Depression and its immediate aftermath, the United States has never endured such a stretch of income stagnation. The tangible hardship this presents to millions of American families is large and pervasive.

WHAT ROLE HAS TRADE PLAYED?

What forces explain this recent poor income performance for so many American workers? At least some of it may reflect the business cycle, which means that earnings should strengthen more broadly as the economy recovers. But almost surely, these weak earnings also reflect structural forces such as global engagement, skill-biased technological change, and evolving labor-market institutions. Anecdotes abound that, in collective bargaining negotiations, union members are regularly faced with demands for wage and benefit concessions because companies have the option of reducing production in the United States and expanding abroad. With the information technology revolution, many workers with even college or nonprofessional master's degrees now face competition from overseas in activities such as business services and programming. And the ongoing integration of world markets may have increased the scale over which highly skilled Americans in activities such as entertainment, finance, and management can operate—leading to higher incomes for those individuals.

The list of plausible trade-related forces affecting U.S. wages in recent years is long, but is characterized by three major factors:

- *Declining political barriers to trade.* The Uruguay Round was the most comprehensive trade agreement ever negotiated. It was concluded in 1994 and member countries implemented it between 1995 and 2004. Since 1995, several hundred bilateral and regional trade agreements have also been concluded, as well as considerable unilateral trade opening. China, now the world's second-biggest economy, joined the World Trade Organization in December 2001. The Information Technology Agreement (ITA)—ratified in 1996 by dozens of countries that collectively account for nearly 95 percent of the world's IT trade—eliminated over the span of several years all world tariffs on hundreds of IT intermediate inputs, capital goods, and final products. And during this time, political barriers have also generally fallen for foreign direct investment.

– *Declining natural barriers to trade.* Since 1995, a major force reducing natural trade barriers has been the Internet. The first major commercial Internet browser, Netscape, had its initial public offering in August 1995. The subsequent explosion of connectivity and communication has been stunning. In many parts of the world, the marginal transmission costs of transporting voice and data have plummeted to near zero. For international trade and investment in services, this revolution has not only reduced the costs of already-traded services but has also vastly expanded the scope of services that can be considered tradable rather than nontradable.

– *GDP growth worldwide.* Overall GDP growth worldwide accelerated dramatically—in particular, growth in middle- and low-income countries such as the BRIC nations of Brazil, Russia, India, and China. From 1990 through 2008, growth in U.S. GDP averaged 2.7 percent—in contrast to the 1990 through 2007 averages of 3.4 percent for the whole world, 4.6 percent for emerging and developing countries as a whole, 6.3 percent in India, and a remarkable 9.9 percent in China. For many of these fast-growing countries, the strongest growth has come since 2000. And in the post-2000 years before the recession, world economic growth was more widely spread than over any period for at least several decades.[23] Overall, this globalized acceleration of economic growth has had a dramatic impact on the distribution and prices of world production.

The visible outcome of these dramatic forces driving globalization has been a surge of international trade and investment, much of it from middle- and low-income countries. For the first time, in 2005, U.S. imports from non–oil developing countries surpassed imports from industrial countries. China stands out: its share of global exports rose from about 3 percent when it joined the WTO to over 10 percent today, and it has now surpassed Germany as the world's largest exporting country.

It is therefore at least plausible that trade and globalization have been major factors in restraining the real earnings of U.S. workers in recent years. Many prominent scholars have conjectured this may be happening. Nobel laureate Paul Krugman's earlier research on trade and wages had, like most others, concluded that trade's impact had been small through the mid-1990s. But he recently suggested this may have changed: "It's no longer safe to assert that trade's impact on the income distribution in wealthy countries is fairly minor. There's a good case that it is big, and getting bigger."[24]

But, unlike the 1970s into the 1990s, this recent period has not been comprehensively examined by economists and other scholars. Researchers now face more difficulty trying to separate forces such as trade, FDI, and technological change. Suppose that a U.S. multinational company establishes a new affiliate in India to provide Internet-enabled back-office accounting support for its U.S. operations. Would the resulting job or wage loss for the company's U.S. workers be attributed to trade, FDI, or technological change? The answer seems to be yes, yes, and yes.

The mix of economic forces accounting for U.S. income pressures is not yet understood, nor is it known how long these pressures may persist. Nonetheless, plausible connections can be made, and it seems reasonable to think that trade has played some role in the post-2000 wage stagnation in America.

THE LABOR MARKET AND VOTER ATTITUDES TOWARD TRADE

The link between individuals' labor-market interests and their policy opinions about globalization is strong. There is a correlation between the years of schooling and attitudes toward trade. For example, in the 1990s, high school graduates were almost twice as likely to support protectionist policies as college graduates.

This divide has reflected both the actual and expected earnings performance of respondents. There are two important points about this link between policy opinions and labor-market performance. First, it does not reflect lack of understanding about the benefits of globalization. Polling data show that large majorities of Americans acknowledge the many benefits of freer trade and investment—lower prices, greater product diversity, a competitive spur to firms. At the same time, however, they express widespread concerns about the pressure on jobs and earnings. Second, public opinion is not divided along sectoral lines. The pressures of globalization permeate the entire economy, extending beyond trade- and investment-exposed industries. If workers in a trad-able sector such as automobiles lose their jobs, they compete for new positions in other sectors, placing downward pressure on wages across the economy.

Recent polls illustrate a broadening of antitrade sentiments that coincides with this labor-market scenario. For instance, a *Wall Street Journal*/NBC News survey published in October 2010 had asked the fol-lowing question over the span of several years: "In general, do you think that free trade agreements between the United States and foreign coun-tries have helped the United States, have hurt the United States, or have not made much of a difference either way?"

When asked this question in December 1999, 39 percent of Ameri-cans said helped and only 30 percent said hurt. By March 2007, consis-tent with the wage pressures over that decade, 26 percent said helped and 48 percent said hurt. And by September 2010, 17 percent said helped and 53 percent said hurt (see Figure 4). The opposition to trade is now surprisingly pervasive across skill and income groups, and fears are also being voiced by highly educated, high-income Americans—precisely those whose real incomes began being pressured around 2000. As the

FIGURE 4: CHANGING PUBLIC OPINION ON TRADE: HAS TRADE HELPED OR HURT THE UNITED STATES?

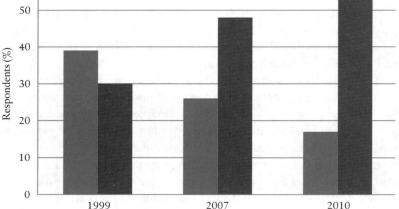

Source: Wall Street Journal/NBC News survey

Wall Street Journal noted, "Even Americans most likely to be winners from trade—upper-income, well-educated professionals, whose jobs are less likely to go overseas and whose industries are often buoyed by demand from international markets—are increasingly skeptical."

Today U.S. policymakers face a public broadly skeptical about whether trade and globalization benefit them personally. U.S. trade policy is unlikely to garner the needed public support unless it can do more to address the source of this skepticism—declining wages and job opportunities for too many Americans.

Revitalizing Trade Negotiations

If the United States is to capture the benefits from a growing world economy for its citizens, and begin to reverse the job loss and income stagnation of the past decade, a new trade negotiating strategy that plays to American strengths is needed. The rapid growth of emerging markets presents an enormous, and still largely untapped, opportunity for gains in exports of U.S.-produced goods and services.

For half a century, the United States led the world in pushing for successively more ambitious agreements to remove barriers to global trade and investment. NAFTA and the Tokyo and Uruguay Rounds of the GATT helped propel the accelerated growth of global trade over the past three decades. The United States has benefited significantly from expanded trade opportunities, the creation of better rules for global commerce, the strengthening of multilateral institutions, and trade-driven development in many poorer countries. Yet since the negotiations that brought China into the WTO in 2001, the fruits of trade negotiations have diminished. The Doha Round, launched in 2001, has now dragged on longer than any other multilateral trade round, and appears unlikely to produce an agreement that offers large economic gains for the United States. U.S. hopes for a Free Trade Area of the Americas (FTAA) to link the United States to Latin America have been shelved; China recently supplanted the United States as Brazil's largest trading partner. The APEC forum goal set in 1994 of negotiating free trade in the region for all advanced economies by 2010 quietly passed with scarcely a notice.

The United States has been active in bilateral negotiations, concluding eleven trade agreements in the past decade, as well as the regional CAFTA. These agreements have met an extremely high standard by not only eliminating tariffs on goods and agricultural products, but also covering intellectual property, investment, government procurement, service sector trade, and regulatory standards including labor and environmental standards. As the president's Export Council recently noted, "U.S. trade agreements can be fairly characterized as representing the 'gold standard' of bilateral and regional agreements."[25] Although ambitious in content and scope, only three of these agreements have been with countries that rank among the top twenty-five U.S. trading partners, and only South Korea is among the top ten.

Ratification delays have been costly as well. South Korea and the European Union (EU) recently approved their bilateral trade agreement, depriving U.S. companies of a head start in one of the most important markets in Asia. The United States also lost that edge in Colombia, where it has seen sharp declines in exports of agricultural goods such as corn, wheat, and soybeans following tariff-lowering deals Colombia concluded with both Brazil and Argentina.[26] Canada will implement its trade deal with Colombia this year, creating further competition for U.S. exports.

The Obama administration's primary negotiating initiative, the Trans-Pacific Partnership, is likely to break new ground on issues such as trade facilitation, harmonizing rules of origin to allow global supply chains to operate more efficiently, restraints on state-owned enterprises, and protection of new forms of intellectual property. Eight countries are currently part of the negotiations with the United States, and Japan, the Philippines, Indonesia, and Thailand have all indicated some interest in being included. These developments are encouraging.

International negotiations are not the only means for liberalizing trade. From 1983 to 2003—the most active period of trade negotiations in history—fully 65 percent of the tariff reductions in developing countries came from unilateral liberalization. The Uruguay Round accounted for another 25 percent, and regional and bilateral agreements the remaining 10 percent.[27]

But trade negotiations allow countries to balance their own concessions with equivalent concessions from other countries. This formula has helped overcome domestic political opposition from heavily protected sectors. Additionally, multilateral negotiations have created rules for international trade that would not have emerged through unilateral liberalization. Countries have locked in tariff reductions and other liberalization measures to protect against backsliding during times of economic distress. The lack of significant trade protectionism during the recent recession was certainly due in part to these binding commitments.[28]

Trade negotiations have also strengthened diplomatic relations between the United States and other countries. It is no coincidence that the first U.S. bilateral FTA was with Israel, its closest ally in the most strategically important region in the world. The United States has since negotiated trade and investment framework agreements and broader trade agreements with a number of important strategic partners in the Middle East, Asia, and Latin America, and it has also used its unilateral trade preference programs to encourage development and strengthen relations with countries in Africa, Latin America, and the Caribbean.

Despite this successful record, however, the limitations to the trade negotiating strategy long embraced by the United States are increasingly evident. On the one hand, the United States remains wedded to pursuing multilateral trade liberalization through massive negotiating rounds that require consensus among many countries in the WTO. As the Doha Round has demonstrated, such consensus is increasingly elusive. The large emerging economies, such as Brazil, India, and China, have resisted market-opening offers consistent with their size and importance in the global economy. And, unlike in past rounds, these countries have enough influence to prevent a successful conclusion to the negotiations. This has pushed the Doha Round to the brink of failure.[29]

On the other hand, the United States has entered numerous bilateral trade agreements. These agreements have been comprehensive, but most have produced only modest economic benefits. Post-NAFTA, U.S. FTA partners account for just under 5.5 percent of total U.S. trade. Additionally, the political challenge of getting these smaller agreements through Congress has been as great as winning support for larger agreements.

Some other countries have pursued more ambitious bilateral and regional trade-negotiating agendas. The EU has entered into negotiations with India, with the countries of the Association of Southeast Asian Nations (ASEAN), as well as with South Korea and Canada, and China has pursued trade links throughout the Asia-Pacific region. These agreements often leave some sensitive sectors, especially in agriculture, out of the negotiations. But for the United States, these deals nonetheless tilt the global market in favor of its largest competitors, leaving U.S.-based production at a disadvantage.

The United States needs a more flexible and varied negotiating strategy that can yield greater market opening in the sectors and countries that promise the largest economic gains. The Task Force believes that the United States should revitalize its trade-negotiating agenda by focusing on the biggest markets and sectors that have the greatest potential for increasing U.S. production of goods and services and for creating additional employment and income in the United States.

SERVICES TRADE

Service companies broadly account for about 85 percent of U.S. employment, and service sector employment has risen steadily even as jobs in manufacturing and agriculture have fallen. Business and professional services such as publishing, software, telecommunications, finance and insurance, real estate, accounting and engineering make up about 25 percent of U.S. employment—more than twice the level of manufacturing.[30] In other areas, such as health services and education, that are increasingly being delivered across borders, the United States has a strong competitive advantage. These are mostly higher-paying jobs, with average wages 22 percent above those in the manufacturing sector. Any trade strategy focused on expanding higher-wage employment needs to seek out opportunities in these higher-end services.

Although only a small portion of services is currently traded, it already accounts for nearly one-third of total U.S. exports, and the tradable portion of the service economy is growing rapidly due to advances in Internet and other communications technologies. U.S. cross-border exports of services grew by more than 85 percent from 2003 to 2010, reaching nearly $550 billion, outpacing the growth of manufacturing exports. The U.S. surplus in services trade grew from $54 billion to $146 billion, compared with the large deficit in goods, which ranged from $500 billion to more than $800 billion over the same period.

The United States also has a strong competitive advantage in technology innovation, information, and media. According to a recent U.S. International Trade Commission (ITC) report, U.S. receipts from intellectual property (IP) royalties and license fees yielded a $64.6 billion trade surplus in 2009.[31] Service exports also declined much less during the recession than manufacturing exports did.[32] The U.S. share of global commercial services exports is nearly 14 percent, almost twice that of its nearest competitor, the United Kingdom. The service

FIGURE 5: U.S. CROSS-BORDER SERVICES TRADE AND SURPLUS,
2000–2010

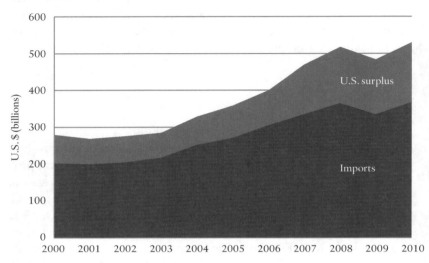

Sources: U.S. Census Bureau, U.S. Bureau of Economic Analysis

sectors are poised for even faster growth as middle-class populations
expand in the developing world. Additionally, opening the U.S. market
to imports of competitive services could help reduce costs and contribute to stronger growth in nontradable sectors and in manufacturing.
Expanding services trade plays to many of the core strengths of the
U.S. economy.

The growth in the tradable portion of the services economy has
raised fears over offshoring, some arguing that millions of services jobs
could move overseas in search of lower wages, as has happened with
some manufacturing employment.[33] J. Bradford Jensen, however, who
has done the most in-depth work on services trade, argues that the tradable portions of the services economy are heavily concentrated in fields
that require higher education, technical sophistication, and creativity,
thus playing to U.S. economic strengths. Those jobs are more similar to
the manufacturing jobs that have remained in the United States in sectors like aircraft, chemicals, and transportation equipment than to the
lower-wage textile and apparel industry jobs that have disappeared.[34]
The rising U.S. trade surplus in services would suggest that the United
States is competitive in these sectors.

Yet though the United States is among the world leaders in many tradable service sectors, services have long been a second- or third-order priority in U.S. trade negotiations. Even some of the most basic building blocks, such as adequate, detailed statistics on trade flows, are woefully underdeveloped in services compared with manufacturing and agriculture.[35] Services negotiations are difficult, often reaching into areas of domestic regulation and competition policies that are complex and politically sensitive. The Uruguay Round failed to do more than require most countries to maintain existing levels of market access for services, and services are the least advanced portion of the Doha Round.

The potential for gains is substantial. The European Commission (EC) has tried to quantify in tariff equivalents the impact of protection in various service sectors, and the results are striking. The EC estimates the tariff equivalents in telecommunications services, for instance, range from 24 percent in developed countries to 50 percent in developing countries—a much higher level of protection than in manufacturing. In transportation the figures are 17 and 27 percent respectively, and in construction 42 and 80 percent.[36] The OECD is engaged in a similar effort to develop a services restrictiveness index to quantify service sector protection as an aid to trade negotiations.[37] Lowering these barriers would yield significant economic benefits for the United States.

REVITALIZING THE WTO

The failure of the Doha Round to progress has been a significant setback for U.S. trade policy. Many issues—from tariff reductions to agricultural subsidies to product safety standards—are best dealt with multilaterally. Further, the WTO dispute settlement system could become increasingly ineffective without an ongoing negotiating process to improve and refine trading rules.

For the United States, which has historically preferred multilateral liberalization over regional and bilateral initiatives, the slow progress of the round has contributed to the overall lethargy in U.S. trade policy. Positive measures are on the table. An agreement could eliminate farm export subsidies and make potentially significant reductions to other trade-distorting agricultural supports. Agreed improvements in trade facilitation would reduce the costs of doing international business. Duty- and quota-free treatment for the least developed countries is a long-standing pledge and would at least go part of the way to fulfilling the Doha Round's development promises. Progress on industrial tariffs is less notable. Both the United States and the EU have made offers that would reduce total duties levied by nearly half, but the biggest developing countries such as Brazil, India, and China oppose further tariff reductions in important sectors such as machinery, chemicals, and electronics.[38]

Despite the difficulties in the negotiations, the best outcome for the United States would still be an ambitious Doha Round agreement that would offset the tariff advantages that European, Canadian, and other foreign companies have gained as a result of the more ambitious bilateral trade negotiations by their governments. But the continued stasis hurts the United States by diverting attention from other trade initiatives and preventing the WTO from being used as a negotiating forum for other issues. Some Task Force members believe that the United States should try to conclude the negotiations as quickly as possible on the most favorable terms; others do not believe such a deal would be substantively justified or would be able to win approval by Congress. But there is a general consensus that the United States needs to get beyond the Doha talks. The future of the WTO does not depend on the success or failure of this particular set of negotiations.

The original vision of the WTO was that it would become a forum for continued negotiations on a broad range of trade issues, not just a vessel for the results of big trade rounds. Issues that could be negotiated through the WTO post-Doha include food and product safety standards; additional liberalization of information, communications, and telecommunications products and services; and the elimination of tariffs and other barriers to trade in environmental goods. Issues on the horizon include the need to set rules for the use of border taxes on carbon or other measures aimed at reducing greenhouse gas emissions and slowing climate change. Bringing China into the WTO government procurement agreement, as it pledged when it acceded to the WTO, should remain a high priority for the United States.

The WTO, as the one negotiating forum that brings together nearly all of the world's countries, has tremendous value both in liberalizing trade and in establishing and enforcing trade rules. Regional or bilateral negotiations are no substitute. The United States should work with other countries to close out the Doha Round and should engage WTO members on a variety of negotiating fronts that reflect U.S. trade priorities.

BILATERAL AND REGIONAL NEGOTIATIONS

Bilateral and regional trade agreements are a second-best approach, and in some cases do little more than divert trade rather than expand trade flows.[39] Further, the proliferation of such agreements has produced increasingly complex rules of origin that raise costs for companies doing business under those arrangements. Nonetheless, tariff disadvantages for U.S.-based production as a result of such agreements can encourage companies to locate facilities outside the United States. Ensuring that U.S. goods do not face tariff penalties or other discriminatory barriers in any of the world's major markets must be a fundamental goal for U.S. trade negotiations.

The United States has set the global standard for comprehensive trade agreements. Although such agreements remain the ideal, some of the countries with the fastest-growing markets are not prepared to enter into such commitments. As a result, U.S.-based production could be disadvantaged. Countries in Asia, for instance, have concluded or are currently negotiating nearly three hundred trade agreements among themselves that exclude the United States. While those deals are far from comprehensive, they nonetheless give advantages to Asian-based production. The EU is well advanced in negotiations with India, and Canada and India launched trade talks in November 2010. Japan, China, and South Korea recently launched FTA negotiations. The United States cannot afford to be left behind, in part because such negotiations often establish the basis for product and other regulatory standards. By allowing the EU, in particular, to gain a first-move advantage, U.S. companies may find themselves forced to conform to European regulatory standards if they are to sell into the world's fastest-growing markets.

U.S. manufacturers are well placed to succeed in these markets if they do not face disadvantageous trade terms. U.S. manufacturing productivity has continued to be extremely strong, and labor productivity in the United States is now well ahead of both Europe and Japan. Although much of the recent gain has come from cost-cutting that reduced employment and held down labor costs, U.S. manufacturers are now poised for employment-generating productivity gains that come from expanding sales volume.[40] The weaker U.S. dollar has also helped, though it remains overvalued versus the Chinese renminbi. But China has been making serious efforts to shrink its trade surplus and to expand both domestic consumption and imports, trends that would benefit U.S. exporters.[41]

The United States cannot afford to wait to seize such opportunities. Many of the world's developing countries are in the midst of building the infrastructures of modern economies—roads, bridges, mass transit, ports and airports, telecommunications and broadband, pipelines, and electricity transmission. All are sectors in which U.S. companies are highly competitive, though they face intense competition from Europe, Japan, Canada, China, and elsewhere.

Finally, in agriculture, rising prices for main food crops are promising record export opportunities and earnings for U.S. farmers. Agricultural exports are forecast to reach $135.5 billion this year, and the trade surplus in farm products is expected to reach $47.5 billion—the largest positive balance in real dollars since the early 1980s.[42] These numbers are being reached in spite of high trade barriers to agricultural imports that remain in most countries. Within a decade, China alone is forecast to buy two-thirds of the world's soybean imports and nearly half of its cotton imports; the United States is the world's largest exporter of each. Such gains, coupled with a flat or shrinking federal budget, could also improve political prospects for deeper cuts to domestic subsidies and other farm income supports, steps that would make it easier to negotiate market-opening deals with some of the large emerging economies.

Although many factors will determine whether the United States remains an attractive base for production in the global market, full access to export opportunities anywhere in the world is a critical variable. The United States must regain its historic leadership on trade opening.

The Task Force believes that the United States should embrace an ambitious trade-negotiating agenda as a clear signal to U.S. and foreign companies, to trading partners, and to all Americans that it sees the expansion of trading opportunities as a critical part of its economic future.

Attracting and Retaining Investment

The policy challenge facing the United States today is not just to create jobs of any kind but instead to create well-paying jobs that will reverse the falling earnings that many Americans have experienced over the past decade. Well-paying jobs tend to be those that boost worker productivity through R&D, capital investment, and international trade. Over much of the twentieth century, multinational companies tended to create these sorts of jobs in the United States.

Attracting more U.S. investment from multinational companies could help expand U.S. trade engagement in ways that benefit more American workers. But the record of the past decade is discouraging. Multinational companies have continued contributing to U.S. productivity growth by expanding capital investment and R&D. But earlier decades of rising U.S. employment in these firms has reversed; in 2009, multinational companies in the United States employed about three million fewer workers than they did in 1999. The United States is losing ground in the global competition for investment by the world's multinational companies, which has negative consequences for economic growth, job creation, and trade expansion.

HOW MULTINATIONAL COMPANIES HAVE HISTORICALLY STRENGTHENED THE U.S. ECONOMY

Historical data for the United States and many other countries have shown that globally engaged companies tend on a number of measures to perform better than purely domestic firms. They are larger, more capital intensive, more skill intensive, and more productive—all of which results in higher wages for workers. Tables 2 and 3 document evidence of the superior performance of U.S. companies that are part of multinational firms.[43]

TABLE 2: PERFORMANCE OF U.S. PARENTS OF U.S.-BASED MULTINATIONAL FIRMS

Activity	Parent Share	Parent Value
Employment	17.80%	$21.1 million
GDP	21.00%	$2.4 trillion
Capital investment	29.20%	$478.8 billion
Imports of goods	33.30%	$707.2 billion
Exports of goods	43.50%	$551.0 billion
R&D	70.30%	$199.1 billion

Source: U.S. Bureau of Economic Analysis

TABLE 3: PERFORMANCE OF U.S. AFFILIATES OF FOREIGN-BASED MULTINATIONAL FIRMS

Activity	Affiliate Share	Affiliate Value
Employment	4.60%	$5.6 million
GDP	6.00%	$670.3 billion
Capital investment	11.40%	$187.5 billion
Imports of goods	26.70%	$566.9 billion
Exports of goods	18.30%	$232.4 billion
R&D	14.30%	$40.5 billion

Source: U.S. Bureau of Economic Analysis

U.S.-based companies that are part of multinational firms account for fewer than 1 percent of all companies. But in 2008 these firms accounted for 22.4 percent of all private-sector jobs, undertook 39.3 percent of all U.S. capital investment, shipped 61.8 percent of all U.S. goods exports, brought in 59.9 percent of all goods imports, and conducted a remarkable 84.6 percent of all U.S. private-sector R&D. For the 26.7 million employees of these multinational companies (MNCs) in 2008, this meant an average annual compensation of $66,733—about 25 percent above the economy-wide average. U.S. affiliates of foreign multinationals have long had substantially higher unionization rates than the rest of the U.S. private sector.[44]

U.S. multinationals have historically played a significant role in driving aggregate U.S. productivity growth, the foundation of rising standards of living. Between 1977 and 2000, multinational firms operating in the United States accounted for more than 75 percent of total U.S. private-sector productivity growth. Moreover, MNCs accounted for all of the post-1995 acceleration in productivity growth in the U.S. private sector.[45]

MNCs have also strengthened the broader U.S. economy. A recent study estimated that the U.S.-parent operations of the typical U.S. MNC buys goods and services from more than six thousand American small businesses, purchases a total of over \$3 billion in inputs from these small-business suppliers, and relies on them for over 24 percent of its total input purchases. Collectively, U.S. parents of U.S. multinationals purchase an estimated \$1.52 trillion in intermediate inputs from U.S. small businesses, which is about 12.3 percent of their total sales.[46]

In short, multinational companies have historically created millions of U.S. jobs based on knowledge creation, capital investment, and international trade—all activities associated with higher compensation and rising overall U.S. productivity. To reverse the income stagnation and job loss of the past decade, the United States needs to create millions of precisely these types of "good jobs at good wages." But the recent evidence is not encouraging.

THE EMPLOYMENT CHALLENGE: FALLING U.S. EMPLOYMENT IN MULTINATIONAL COMPANIES IN RECENT YEARS

Until roughly 2000, multinational companies' presence in the U.S. economy was stable or, by many measures, expanding. Through the 1990s, U.S.-headquartered MNCs created new jobs at a faster rate than the rest of the private sector. The same was true for the U.S. affiliates of foreign MNCs, whose total U.S. employment more than doubled from 2.6 million in 1987 to 5.6 million in 2002. In the past decade, however, the number of U.S. jobs in these companies has been falling. Tables 4 and 5 report total U.S. employment in MNCs over the 1990s and 2000s— where 2009 is the most recent year of preliminary data available.[47]

What forces explain these job losses? These companies did not shrink. From 1999 through 2008, U.S. parents saw their sales increase by 46.1 percent and boosted their R&D spending by 57.7 percent. And

TABLE 4: EMPLOYMENT IN U.S. PARENTS AND FOREIGN
AFFILIATES OF U.S.-BASED MULTINATIONAL FIRMS (MILLIONS)

Year	U.S. Parents	Foreign Affiliates
1989	19.6	5.2
1994	19.3	5.8
1999	24	7.9
2004	22.4	9
2007	22.8	10.4
2009	21.1	10.3

Source: U.S. Bureau of Economic Analysis

TABLE 5: EMPLOYMENT IN U.S. AFFILIATES OF FOREIGN-BASED
MULTINATIONAL FIRMS (MILLIONS)

Year	U.S. Affiliates
1992	3.9
1997	4.4
2002	5.6
2007	5.6
2009	5.2

Source: U.S. Bureau of Economic Analysis

falling employment did not drive down wages. In contrast to nearly
all U.S. workers during the 2000s, workers at U.S.-headquartered
MNCs saw average real compensation rise by 7.1 percent from 2000
through 2008.[48]

This recent trend of falling U.S. employment in MNCs has not yet
been comprehensively examined by economists and other scholars. One
force seems to have been the business cycle—in particular, the historic
drop in business activity during the Great Recession. Another factor
is strong productivity gains. In manufacturing, for example, growth in
labor productivity during the 2000s far outpaced productivity growth
in the rest of the U.S. economy, which contributed to employment
declines in U.S. manufacturing.[49]

A third force cited by some is the exporting of jobs to foreign affiliates. But academic research to date has found little evidence of this.
Instead, it has found that expansion abroad by these companies has generally supported their U.S. operations, and that foreign-affiliate activity
usually complements, rather than substitutes for, U.S. activities.[50]

One force that explains the growth of MNC jobs abroad has surely
been much faster economic growth overseas. Indeed, 60.9 percent of
the 2000 though 2007 employment increase in foreign affiliates was
accounted for by just three industries—retail trade, business administration and support services, and food and accommodation services—
the type of businesses where reaching foreign customers necessarily
happens through affiliates, not exports, and where foreign expansion
tends to complement parent activity, not substitute for it.

Whatever the causes, the trend is alarming. Multinational companies
have long been among the United States' most dynamic, productive,
and trade intensive. At a time when America needs to create millions of
well-paying jobs, it is facing ever-tougher competition to attract these
multinational companies that could help solve its employment crisis.

The policy challenges here are many and will be difficult to meet. Signs
indicate that multinational companies are again interested in expanding
here. The Boston Consulting Group recently predicted a manufacturing renaissance given falling wages in the United States and rising wages
in China that have reduced the Chinese cost advantage. When access to
skilled labor and transportation costs are factored in, more companies
are concluding that expansion in the United States makes sense.[51]

But the United States currently lacks a strategic vision for attracting
and expanding investment that will create higher-wage jobs. Instead,
policies are fragmented and unfocused not just on trade and investment, but also on a broader set of competitiveness issues that include
tax policy, education, and infrastructure. In a recent report, McKinsey
conducted in-depth interviews with senior executives from twenty-six
of the largest and best-known U.S.-headquartered multinationals. The
message was sobering. They worry that many current U.S. policies—
such as high and complex corporate taxation, limits on skilled immigration, and bureaucratic hurdles and inconsistencies—handicap their
companies, compromising the future ability of the United States to
attract corporate investment, R&D, and jobs.[52]

The biggest concern for leading companies is the U.S. statutory corporate tax rate, which at 35 percent stands today as one of the world's
highest. Despite various loopholes that make the effective rate much

lower for many companies, the U.S. corporate tax system still inhibits hiring and investment in U.S. firms, large and small alike. U.S.-headquartered companies are also taxed on their worldwide income, whereas most other advanced countries tax corporations only on domestic earnings. One result is that U.S. MNCs generally leave their overseas earnings offshore to be reinvested, rather than repatriating those funds and paying the high corporate rate, which works directly against investment in the United States.

The United States faces a further competitive disadvantage because many of its largest trading partners and competitors, including Canada, Japan, and China—indeed, every other member of the OECD—rely heavily on value-added taxes (VATs) to raise revenue. Under long-standing international trade rules, VATs are a boon to both export and import competitiveness because they are levied on imported goods and rebated on exported goods.

There are many other areas of concern. America's educational upgrading has slowed dramatically in the past forty years as it has accelerated in dozens of other countries. The median U.S. worker today has a high school degree and a little over one year of higher education, a level that workers in dozens of other countries are rapidly approaching or exceeding. America's infrastructure is crumbling; in its 2009 *Report Card for America's Infrastructure*, the American Society of Civil Engineers assigned a grade of D for the quality of U.S. infrastructure overall, even as dozens of other countries continue to deepen their infrastructure networks.

In the short term, certain policy changes could surely boost the attractiveness of the United States as a location for globally engaged employment and production. This report addresses some of these, including greater trade liberalization in areas of U.S. comparative advantage, a new initiative to organize and expand U.S. investment promotion policies, and significant reforms to U.S. corporate taxation. Smarter U.S. policies toward international trade and investment clearly can and should be one part of this constellation. But they will not be a panacea.

The Task Force believes that a critical component of a successful U.S. trade policy needs to be a complementary U.S. investment policy that aims to attract, grow, and expand the employment and related activities of global multinational companies on which much of the global trading system is built.

Bolstering Trade Enforcement

Inadequate enforcement of trade rules can have lasting detrimental consequences for U.S.-based production and the U.S. workforce. The United States needs to become a more desirable place to locate production of goods and services. But if overseas competitors are playing by a different set of rules, that goal is extremely difficult to realize. If foreign competitors are heavily subsidized through government intervention, for example, U.S. companies may simply be unable to find the productivity improvements and cost savings needed to overcome the disadvantage. The result is a loss of otherwise competitive companies and industries in the United States or the relocation of increasing portions of the global supply chain outside the United States.

Effective trade enforcement is vital to restoring public confidence. One reason for the growing public skepticism toward trade is the widespread perception that some other countries are not playing by the rules. Unless Americans are persuaded that the rules of the trade game are not tilted against them, it will be nearly impossible to find public support for a more ambitious policy of market opening around the world.

Until the creation of the WTO in 1994, the United States relied primarily on its domestic trade laws and the threat of unilateral trade sanctions as enforcement tools. Most actions were taken as a result of complaints brought by specific U.S. companies whose interests were harmed by restrictions on exports or by import competition. But in the modern era of globally integrated companies and binding dispute settlement, new approaches are needed.

The Task Force believes the United States needs to modernize the way it handles trade enforcement. Enforcement today requires integrating WTO dispute settlement, negotiated resolutions, and more effective use of trade laws into a coherent strategy for ensuring that U.S.-based production does not face unfair competitive disadvantages.

Defining what constitutes an unfair disadvantage is extremely difficult in the abstract. Each country has its own mix of labor costs, tariff and nontariff barriers to imports, investment restrictions, government regulations, local content rules, subsidies, and taxation policies that offer differing advantages and disadvantages to productive activities located in its territory. The U.S. government has tried to use trade negotiations to minimize these disparities, including pushing for enforcement of core labor and environmental standards. Such standards are important both because they help equalize the conditions of international competition and because they promote other values that matter to Americans, such as environmental protection and improved working conditions.

The goal of trade enforcement should be to ensure that U.S. trading partners abide fully by the trade commitments they have freely accepted. If the U.S. government fails to negotiate rules that help the U.S. economy, then the proper response is to negotiate better rules. If the rules are sound and the United States is losing ground, then the proper response is to improve the ability of U.S. firms and workers to compete through domestic measures, such as better education and workforce training, investment in R&D, improvements in infrastructure, reasonable controls on health-care costs, and sound tax and regulatory policies. But when the United States is losing ground because other countries are not upholding rules they freely negotiated, the proper response is more effective enforcement. Maintaining a system of rules-based global trade requires the capacity, willingness, and desire by the U.S. government to enforce the trade rules.

THE CHALLENGE OF ENFORCEMENT

The good news about the global trading system is that most countries, most of the time, live within the rules. This is no small achievement. The recent deep recession could well have resulted in a spate of protectionist measures in response. Yet the number of new trade-restricting measures has been small, affecting only a tiny fraction of global trade.[53]

But as global trading relationships have deepened over the past half century, effective enforcement of trade agreements has become increasingly difficult. The earliest GATT agreements, which reduced tariffs, were easy to monitor, though no binding procedures for resolving disputes were in place. The later expansion of the multilateral trading system to cover areas such as intellectual property, subsidies, food and product safety regulations, and government procurement was intended to ensure that rewards would accrue to the workers and companies producing the best products at the lowest prices, rather than to those benefiting from government support or discriminatory regulation. But those trading rules are far more difficult to enforce.

To take just one example, WTO dispute settlement cases were launched in 2004 to determine whether the world's largest aircraft makers, Airbus and Boeing, had received improper subsidies from governments in Europe and the United States. Seven years later, the final decisions have only recently been issued (the answer was yes in both cases, though the subsidy was much larger for Airbus).

The rise of economic competitors in which the state plays a greater role in market competition exacerbates the enforcement problem. WTO rules were written largely by countries in which private or shareholder-owned companies are the primary economic actors. The question of the appropriate role of government has long created trade disputes and was not resolved by the creation of the WTO.

The high-profile trade clashes between the United States and Japan in the 1980s and early 1990s largely concerned Japanese government–directed measures that protected its market from otherwise competitive imports of U.S. autos, auto parts, medical devices, semiconductors, and beef, to name just a few sectors. Many of these practices were not explicitly prohibited, but they nonetheless harmed U.S. companies selling into the Japanese market or competing with Japanese exporters in the United States or in third markets.[54] Finally, the enforcement challenge has been exacerbated by the growth of truly global companies. U.S. trade enforcement has long been driven by specific companies seeking to remove barriers to exports or block unfairly traded imports. But global companies may be reluctant to pursue either of those remedies, preferring to deal with obstacles through direct investment overseas rather than to fight to expand exports from a U.S. base or protect a domestic market from import competition. This situation requires a more active U.S. government role in choosing and pursuing enforcement priorities than was necessary in the past.

THE EMERGING MARKETS PROBLEM

The enforcement challenge posed today by China and some other emerging markets is especially difficult. Although China has embraced more open trade and investment, the state apparatus remains heavily enmeshed in the economy. Increasingly over the past five years, the Chinese government has used an array of market-distorting measures to lower costs for Chinese firms. This is especially the case in sectors dominated by state-owned enterprises (SOEs)—which include aviation, energy, shipping, chemicals, IT, and telecommunications—where the government is trying to nurture companies that will succeed in global markets.[55] By various estimates, Chinese SOEs make up about half of all Chinese industrial assets.[56]

In its latest five-year plan, China has explicitly targeted seven "strategic emerging industries" and pledged $1.5 trillion in various forms of government support for those sectors. Evidence also indicates that China's SOEs at times have made purchasing and investment decisions based not on commercial considerations, but rather in an effort to advance the Chinese government's political or industrial policy goals. This runs directly counter to commitments China made in its accession agreement to the WTO.[57]

Much of the public attention has focused on Beijing's efforts to suppress the value of its currency, the renminbi, to encourage exports. But the artificially depressed currency is only one of a host of measures the Chinese government uses to support its export sector or to protect domestic firms from competition. These include access to below-market cost financing, discriminatory government procurement, export restraints, antitrust immunities, restrictions on foreign investment, and discriminatory standards and other regulations. These measures can be particularly damaging in service sectors where the United States is highly competitive, including credit card payment processing, insurance, and delivery services. A December 2010 USTR report to Congress on China's compliance with its WTO obligations noted "a troubling trend towards increased state intervention in the Chinese economy in recent years."[58]

Intellectual property violations also remain widespread. The economic costs to the United States continue to grow as readily copied products—from software to digital entertainment—make up a growing share of the U.S. economy. For instance, the U.S. ITC recently reported that if intellectual property rights (IPR) protection in China were improved to a level comparable to that in the United States, net U.S. employment could increase by 2.1 million full-time equivalent workers, U.S. exports of goods and services (including receipt of royalties and license fees) could increase by approximately $21 billion, and U.S. sales to majority-owned affiliates in China could increase by approximately $88 billion.[59]

Most U.S. companies doing business in China have little confidence that the domestic judicial system will protect their intellectual property; domestic enforcement efforts remain token at best. Moreover, Chinese IPR infringement is still rampant across nearly all sectors despite the fact that China's IPR laws generally prohibit such infringement. As a result, U.S. companies often find themselves forced to compete with Chinese companies that have unfairly lowered their input costs by having misappropriated critical U.S. innovations and technologies.

China is hardly alone in using such measures to discourage foreign competitors. Several of the countries in the TPP negotiations, including Singapore, Malaysia, Vietnam, Peru, and Chile, have a long history of significant state involvement in the economy. The most recent USTR report on IP violations cited forty-two countries for failure to adequately protect U.S. intellectual property.[60]

In other sectors, U.S. telecommunications companies have never made serious inroads in the Mexican market, despite the ostensible opening of that market through NAFTA, largely because of Mexican government regulations that favor domestic providers.[61] Preferential government treatment in such sectors as insurance, banking, and international express delivery for the *Japan Post* has similarly limited opportunities for foreign competitors in Japan. And Malaysia maintains a web of import restrictions, government subsidies, and foreign investment restrictions to protect its domestic auto industry from competition.[62]

The United States is certainly not without its own trade agreement violations. But it is nonetheless true that the United States generally faces a broader and more challenging array of trade obstacles abroad than most foreign companies face in selling to the U.S. market.

THE WANING OF TRADITIONAL
TRADE ENFORCEMENT TOOLS

The traditional enforcement tools on which the United States once relied have become either illegal or unviable, or both. Historically, three mechanisms were used:

- negotiations with trading partners, backed by the threat of unilateral trade sanctions if discriminatory practices were not removed;
- the trade remedy laws, which allow companies and workers to petition for import protection if they are harmed by imports that are government subsidized or sold below cost in an effort to gain market share; and
- so-called gray measures, such as voluntary export restraints (VERs), in which the United States pressured trading partners to restrict exports of certain goods.

None of these mechanisms is effective today. In the Uruguay Round negotiations, the United States largely agreed to end unilateral trade sanctions in exchange for the WTO dispute settlement system, in which impartial tribunals can issue binding rulings on violations of WTO rules. U.S. trade remedy laws have become less useful as well. The number of antidumping and countervailing duty (AD/CVD) cases has been dropping steadily over the past decade, despite the deep recession that would normally have triggered an increase in such measures.[63] This decline has come even though changes to rules in recent years have made it easier for U.S. producers to seek tariffs on competitive imports.[64] In August 2010 the Obama administration announced more than a dozen revisions to AD/CVD laws, each aimed at helping U.S. companies win relief against unfairly traded imports.[65]

The use of antidumping and countervailing duty measures has declined in most advanced economies. In the late 1990s, for instance, between 3.5 percent and 5 percent of all imports into developed countries faced some sort of temporary tariff; by 2007 that figure had fallen in half. In contrast, trade covered by such measures in the fastest-growing developing economies—including China, Brazil, Argentina, India, and Turkey—rose from near zero in the mid-1990s to some 4 percent by 2007.[66] Trade law protection for U.S. companies has waned at precisely the time when trade law barriers to U.S. exports are growing in developing countries.[67]

The third traditional enforcement tool, the negotiation of export restraints, was also abolished as a result of the Uruguay Round negotiations in favor of strengthened safeguards provisions to allow countries to deal with import surges. But the United States has generally made only limited use of safeguards, and those actions have nearly all been found to violate WTO rules.[68] In summary, each of the traditional trade enforcement tools used by the United States is either no longer available or no longer particularly effective. The United States must find new ways to enforce trade rules effectively using a different arsenal of measures.

WTO DISPUTE SETTLEMENT

The creation of the WTO dispute settlement system is one of the most impressive achievements in the history of efforts to build cooperation across borders. For the United States, the new system was a calculated gamble. As the world's biggest market, the United States had more power than any other country to get its way in trade disputes by threatening to block imports, and thus had much to lose by foreclosing that option. But, as a country that has largely tried to abide by its trade obligations, the United States had a great deal to gain by creating a legal mechanism that would strongly encourage compliance and permit sanctions against other countries if they failed to uphold their commitments.

Since the system was launched in January 1995, more than four hundred disputes have been initiated. It has been, as the former chairman of the WTO's Appellate Body, James Bacchus, has written, "by far the busiest international dispute settlement system in all of history."[69] The United States alone has been complainant or a respondent in more than two hundred cases, and smaller, developing countries are increasingly bringing more cases as well. And the system has delivered results. In nearly 90 percent of those cases, a dispute settlement panel or the Appellate Body found that some violation of trade commitments had occurred. In nearly every case, countries have complied with those rulings without facing the trade sanctions that can result from noncompliance.[70]

The record of U.S. success in WTO cases against China in particular is encouraging. The United States was cautious in pursuing WTO cases in the years immediately following China's accession, offering China a grace period to achieve full compliance with the rules. Though the United States filed the first ever WTO dispute case against China, it brought only two cases against China in the first five years after China's WTO accession. But since the deadline for China to achieve full compliance with its WTO obligations by December 31, 2006, the United States has become more aggressive in pursuing cases, bringing eleven challenges in Geneva.[71] Despite the generally positive U.S. experience with WTO dispute settlement, however, the system has significant shortcomings, including the following:

- The long time required to bring and resolve cases so that even a favorable ruling may be a pyrrhic victory because the economic damage has already been done. Although the U.S. case against Airbus has been upheld at both the panel and Appellate Body levels, for example, subsidies for Airbus have already helped the company capture half the global market for large civil aircraft.

- Compliance with WTO rulings can be difficult to monitor and assess. Countries often make the smallest changes possible to existing trade practices in order to come into technical compliance with rulings.

- U.S. companies are reluctant to be seen as encouraging or supporting WTO cases, especially against China, fearing that it could lead to retaliatory measures that would harm their existing market access or benefit competitors.[72]

- The WTO system deals reasonably well with trade violations in specific sectors or industries, but has a harder time dealing with larger systemic problems that can lead to competitive disadvantages. These include national standards of different sorts, some types of government subsidies, IP violations, SOE activity that is motivated by factors other than commercial considerations, and currency manipulation.[73]

- No negotiating process is currently in place that would allow for changes to the rules in cases where countries believe the panels have wrongly interpreted the Uruguay Round agreements, or where the rules are inadequate to resolve a particular dispute. In the absence of any procedure for updating the agreements, the dispute process is likely to become less and less applicable to the different sorts of trade frictions that will arise in the future.

Although the WTO dispute settlement system has brought many gains to the United States and other countries, the United States needs to find ways to use that process more effectively, and to initiate negotiations that could help improve those procedures.

BILATERAL NEGOTIATIONS

Over the years, the United States has established a number of formal bilateral processes for addressing trade frictions. These have included the U.S.-Japan Structural Impediments Initiative, the U.S.-EU summit process, and the Security and Prosperity Partnership (SPP) with Canada and Mexico. The idea behind each was to allow for detailed discussions on trade-related issues not readily dealt with through the WTO, NAFTA, or other trade forums. These include many regulatory matters, customs facilitation, competition policy, and other issues that often reach quite deeply into domestic politics and regulation.

In recent years, however, these bilateral processes have waned in importance. The U.S.-EU summits used to be regular, biannual meetings, and the need for deliverables helped drive an ongoing trade-negotiating process. They have since become more sporadic and less focused.[74] There is similarly no regular summit process between the United States and either Canada or Mexico, its first- and third-largest export markets, respectively. The SPP was supposed to provide political impetus for efforts to deepen North American integration, but instead it became bogged down in political controversy and dominated by post-9/11 security concerns.[75]

The United States and Japan similarly no longer have a formal trade-negotiating structure in place. The most intensive bilateral negotiating process currently in place is with China. The Joint Commission on Cooperation and Trade (JCCT) has become the forum for negotiating on discrete trade and investment issues, and the Strategic and Economic Dialogue (SED), launched in 2006, deals with higher-level strategic and economic concerns, including regional stability in Asia, macroeconomic imbalances, and currency valuations.

What can be achieved through such bilateral negotiations is limited. The U.S. history with Japan indicates that the greatest progress comes when outside pressure helps reinforce existing domestic pressure for change. If the demands are seen as legitimate and promise to help with domestic economic problems, they have a far greater chance of success.[76] A fundamental purpose of such negotiations is to find mutual interests not previously recognized. U.S. trading partners are most likely to remove market barriers when they see it to be in their economic interest rather than under the threat of sanctions.

The bilateral (or trilateral, in the case of NAFTA) negotiations process respects the reality that the biggest players in the world trading system—China, the EU, Japan, and the United States, as well as Canada and Mexico—are more likely to respond to persuasion or to negotiated trade-offs than to aggressive sanctions threats. China, for example, has shown willingness to respond to U.S. concerns in the context of high-level dialogue. At the January 2011 summit meeting in Washington between Barack Obama and Hu Jintao, China agreed to what could be significant changes in its "indigenous innovation" policy, by pledging that there would no longer be special preference for domestically developed technologies in procurement by the Chinese government. The results are still unclear, however; U.S. firms want to see results in terms of sales before they will declare success.

Promoting U.S. Trade Competitiveness

The United States has not made consistent, concerted efforts to boost sales of U.S.-made goods and services abroad, and partly as a result has lost ground to countries with governments more focused on success in global markets. Certainly, the role of any government in export success will always be modest. In the United States, trade is carried out largely by the private sector, and the government role is a supporting one. But many other governments, in economies similarly led by the private sector, do far more to support their companies in identifying and exploiting market opportunities. Governments can play a catalyzing role by collecting and disseminating information, providing advice and logistical support to smaller U.S. exporters, assisting with export financing where appropriate, and actively promoting U.S. goods and services through trade missions and other tools.

With the fastest growth now taking place in emerging markets that are often unfamiliar to U.S. companies, the U.S. government needs to expand its trade promotion efforts. The Obama administration's National Export Initiative has sent an important signal that the U.S. government is committed to supporting exports of U.S.-produced goods and services. The administration has set an ambitious target of doubling exports by the end of 2014.

The first step is to benchmark U.S. trade promotion efforts against those of its major competitors. In most respects, the United States does not appear to measure up well. As an example, export financing is often necessary to secure contracts in such sectors as electricity generation, rail and aerospace, and other large infrastructure projects in which U.S. firms face tough competition from Europe, Japan, Canada, and increasingly China and Brazil. Government-backed financing for exports supports only a small fraction of total exports, but such assistance can be particularly crucial for U.S. companies competing for large contracts in the developing world, where guaranteed financing can provide a significant competitive advantage.

U.S.-government export financing through the Export-Import Bank has grown from $14 billion in 2008 to $25 billion in 2010 and is a high priority of the current administration. Yet the U.S. effort is still small compared to many of its largest competitors. Less than 2 percent of U.S. capital goods exports receive Export Credit Agency (ECA) support, compared with nearly 3 percent in Germany, 6 percent in France, and 7 to 8 percent in Canada.[77] And, in 2010, for the first time, export financing by India, China, and Brazil combined exceeded that of the G7 economies.[78] Brazilian and Chinese companies receive ten times more export financing as a percentage of GDP than U.S. companies.[79]

These countries are not signatories to the OECD Arrangement on Export Credits, which restricts the use of financial subsidies to encourage exports, leaving their governments free to offer export financing terms that undercut competitors, including the United States. The Export-Import Bank announced recently that it would match Chinese financing for a sale of locomotives that General Electric is trying to win in Pakistan, using a provision of the OECD arrangement that allows countries to match noncompliant financing. Further, U.S. export financing has been limited by rigid domestic content requirements and outdated requirements that U.S.-flagged vessels be used for shipping goods financed with export credit support. The Export-Import Bank has set a threshold of 85 percent U.S.-generated content before it will offer full backing for an export contract, though it will support 100 percent of the domestic content of any contract.

In a world of global supply chains, rigid adherence to an arbitrary threshold may discourage using the United States as the main supply center for exports of products that require input from multiple countries. The chief criteria for determining support should be the creation of high-value jobs in the United States.

Consider the effort to promote exports in China, the market that offers perhaps the biggest prospects for expanding U.S. sales. The American Chamber of Commerce in Shanghai, which represents U.S. companies doing business in China, reported recently, "U.S. companies are in a solid position to compete in China but run up against overseas competitors, especially from Europe and Asia, which enjoy well-established government trade promotion support. The result: the U.S. punches far below its weight in exports compared to other large developed countries."[80]

Germany provides a telling comparison. Selling German products is a priority at the highest levels of the government—German chancellor

Angela Merkel has led four trade missions to China to secure contracts for German exporters. The German government maintains four large offices in China to assist small and medium-sized business in identifying and capitalizing on export opportunities. Overall, Germany spends twice as much as the United States on export promotion as a percentage of its GDP. Partly as a result, Germany exports almost two-thirds as much to China as does the United States, even though its economy is only one-quarter the size of the U.S. economy.[81]

Under the NEI, the Obama administration has stepped up efforts in several important areas of export promotion. President Obama has used overseas trips to promote exports of U.S. goods, including on recent visits to India and Brazil. The administration has increased export financing substantially. The White House is also moving forward to develop a strategic export plan that targets specific countries and sectors that offer the greatest export opportunities and develop plans for removing the major trade impediments U.S. companies face.[82] The Task Force recognizes that these initiatives are positive and should be continued and expanded.

Other initiatives could also help support export growth. The administration, for example, is in the midst of a large-scale effort to overhaul U.S. export control laws that restrict the sale of certain goods overseas on national security grounds. Those restrictions cost U.S. firms billions of dollars in lost exports each year. The initiative, announced in August 2009, would aim to streamline U.S. restrictions on exports to ensure that they are focused on goods that raise genuine national security concerns and do not inhibit exports of competitive U.S. products, especially in high-technology sectors.

Finally, the administration has launched an effort to reconfigure the trade-related agencies of the U.S. government to better support the export initiative. Given the urgency of the issues on the U.S. trade agenda, the Task Force would caution against any major reorganization of the trade-related agencies. The danger is that a formal reorganization effort would distract from other, more meaningful efforts to enhance U.S. trade performance, and could delay initiatives that would do more to bolster export performance. Although additional resources are needed to better carry out the government's trade and investment functions, the Task Force does not believe that reorganization should be an immediate priority.

Encouraging Development Through Trade

Since the early 1980s, in part as a result of the dismantling of trade barriers worldwide, reductions in global poverty have been dramatic and sustained. In the early 1980s, more than half of those living in developing countries were in extreme poverty; by 2005 this proportion was down to one-quarter and has been falling sharply since. In the past five years alone, even in the face of a global recession, the numbers living in extreme poverty have by best estimates fallen from 1.3 billion to fewer than 900 million. As the authors of the recent Brookings Institution study that made this estimate put it, "Poverty reduction of this magnitude is unparalleled in history; never before have so many people been lifted out of poverty over such a brief period of time."[83]

The United States has been the largest consumer market for exports from many of the countries that have seen the biggest reductions in poverty, including China, Bangladesh, Pakistan, and Vietnam. In the Center for Global Development's annual Commitment to Development Index, the United States ranks just seventeenth of twenty-two rich countries in adopting policies that benefit the poorest countries, and it has particularly low scores in providing foreign aid. But U.S. trade policies ranked highly due to the openness of the U.S. market to imports.[84] With the U.S. federal budget facing what is likely to be years of reductions or slow growth, the importance of U.S. trade policy in fostering development will only be further magnified.

Many developing countries still face high trade barriers on their exports to the United States, however. Agricultural products in which developing countries are most competitive—from cotton to sugar to orange juice—compete with U.S. products that enjoy generous subsidies, high tariffs, or quota protection. The highest U.S. manufacturing tariffs are in labor-intensive products, such as apparel and shoes. As a result, a country like Vietnam—which exported $13 billion in goods and services to the United States in 2009—paid slightly more in tariffs to the U.S. Treasury than Germany, which exported more than $72 billion to the United States that year.[85]

Such imbalances can be particularly damaging for countries in which, for strategic or political reasons, the United States has a strong interest in promoting development. Muslim-majority countries that are struggling with domestic radicalism, such as Pakistan, Indonesia, and Egypt, face some of the highest barriers in exporting to the United States.[86]

The United States has tried to offset some of these trade barriers by creating preference programs that reduce or eliminate import tariffs for certain products from the world's poorest countries. The major programs include the Generalized System of Preferences, the Caribbean Basin Initiative (CBI), the Andean Trade Preference Act, and the African Growth and Opportunity Act (AGOA). Unlike votes on trade agreements, which have become increasingly narrow and partisan, strong support remains for preference programs.

Investing in countries that have developing middle classes also helps create stability and demand for U.S. products and services, and the United States has enjoyed benefits in terms of its own exports. Since the enactment of the ATPA, for instance, the percentage of U.S. exports going to the four ATPA countries—Peru, Bolivia, Ecuador, and Colombia—has doubled, from 0.9 percent to 1.8 percent.[87] The United States has also been able to pioneer provisions in these arrangements that strongly encourage the beneficiary countries to uphold higher standards for the protection of workers' rights and the environment.

Despite these benefits, the preference programs are in practice often quite limited. The United States excludes many products that raise domestic import sensitivities, often precisely those in which those countries are the most competitive—agricultural goods and labor-intensive manufactured products.

The preference programs are also extended unilaterally, which means they can be withdrawn by the United States at any time. In early 2011, Congress allowed both the GSP and ATPA programs to lapse. If these programs are not renewed retroactively, importers of products from the affected countries will face steep tariff payments. These preference programs have demonstrated their value both in encouraging development and in advancing U.S. foreign policy goals and should be renewed promptly and maintained without lapses in the future.

The United States needs to take a broader approach to using trade as a development tool. For the poorest countries, the certainty of duty-free treatment on exports of the full range of their goods would offer a stability lacking in the current programs. The United States could also look at new measures to encourage U.S. companies to invest in nonextractive sectors to help create jobs and opportunities in these countries. It should also encourage these countries to embrace broader market-opening measures that would encourage improved productivity in the domestic, nontradable sectors of these economies, providing a greater spur to growth than would be possible under a purely export-oriented strategy.

Although the poorest countries offer long-term potential as markets for goods and services, they need to be treated quite differently under U.S. trade policy than countries rapidly moving their populations into the middle class. The United States should maintain and expand on its tradition of offering nonreciprocal access to imports from the poorest countries and taking steps to prepare and encourage these countries to embrace broader market opening.

Comprehensive Adjustment
Assistance for Workers

The U.S. labor market has long been extremely dynamic. Even before the pressures of the recent recession, jobs were appearing and disappearing at high rates. In 2007, for example, private-sector employment expanded by about nine hundred thousand jobs. But this net increase masked the far more dramatic shifts below the surface; the economy that year created about thirty million jobs but lost roughly twenty-nine million. What that means is that, based on an average of four forty-hour work weeks a month, about twenty-five thousand jobs were being destroyed and created every hour that the United States was open for business.

Economic change and adjustment often present real costs to American workers, communities, and firms. Evidence of the costs of involuntary job loss is considerable. About 65 percent of displaced workers find new full-time jobs—but at an average wage loss of 13 to 17 percent. And this average disguises a wide range of experiences: 36 percent secured similar or higher earnings, whereas 25 percent accepted losses of 30 percent or more. In the recent recession, the surge in long-term unemployment has been especially troubling—more than two years since the recession, nearly 50 percent of America's unemployed had been without a job for twenty-seven weeks or longer.

International trade is only one of the forces driving this dynamic reallocation of people, capital, and ideas to emerging business opportunities. Technological change, seasonal business patterns, shifting customer tastes, and many other forces are also at work. Indeed, the vast majority of worker separations are driven by forces other than trade. For example, survey data from the Bureau of Labor Statistics show that in layoffs of fifty or more people between 1996 and 2004, less than 3 percent were attributable to import competition or overseas relocation.

Current U.S. labor-market programs are well intentioned but, because of their design, are inadequate to cope with U.S. labor-market pressures. This is not surprising because current programs were designed in and for another age. Unemployment insurance (UI) was introduced in the early 1930s but has not changed in any fundamental way since then. UI benefits were designed to supplement a worker's salary until the individual was rehired by his or her previous employer. Today, the challenges facing unemployed workers are often much more involved: matching with a new employer, often in a new industry; upgrading or learning new skills; and coping with lost benefits, especially health care.

Trade Adjustment Assistance faces similar problems. Created in the early 1960s and designed to supplement UI, TAA was intended to assist workers displaced by stronger competition from imports. It was expanded in 1993 to account for shifts in production from the United States to Mexico with implementation of NAFTA.

Today, however, rather than facing a one-time adjustment to new levels of import competition, firms and workers face continual adjustment as new technologies and competitors, both domestic and foreign, make existing capital equipment and skills obsolete. With the exception of a small wage-loss insurance program for workers over the age of fifty that is difficult to qualify for, TAA offers adjustment assistance solely to workers who seek retraining, rather than assisting those with the manifold adjustment challenges they face today. Most workers in transition find TAA's current benefits inadequate or inappropriate for their needs: in recent years, fewer than 25 percent of certified workers actually take TAA benefits.

The irony is that, despite the relatively small role that international trade plays in U.S. labor-market dislocations, TAA tends to dominate discussions of how government policy can mitigate the human costs of adjustment. Given the breadth of challenges facing today's U.S. labor market, what is clearly needed is a stronger safety net that assists workers in transition, regardless of the reason they find themselves moving from one job to another.

Reviving Trade Negotiating Authority

No issue has been more divisive in recent years than the question of the president's authority to negotiate and implement trade agreements. The U.S. Constitution divides authority with respect to trade agreements between the president and Congress. It grants to Congress the power to "regulate commerce with foreign nations" and to "lay and collect taxes, duties, imposts, and excises" but reserves for the president exclusive power to negotiate treaties and international agreements.[88] The Trade Act of 1974 created special procedural rules for the consideration of trade agreements, informally known as fast track and later renamed Trade Promotion Authority. As the Senate Finance Committee report that accompanied the 1974 trade act noted, "Our negotiators cannot be expected to accomplish the negotiating goals . . . if there are no reasonable assurances that the negotiated agreements would be voted up-or-down on their merits."[89]

Under the procedures approved in 1974, Congress agreed to consider trade agreements on an expedited schedule and to vote those agreements up or down without amendment. In exchange, it has promulgated extensive and often specific instructions for what should be included in those agreements and how it and private interests should be consulted during negotiation.

This worked well initially. Two major GATT agreements, the Tokyo Round and the Uruguay Round, as well as the U.S.-Canada FTA and NAFTA, were approved by Congress under the fast track procedure. Fast track authority was renewed several times by Congress with strong bipartisan majorities. But, over time, TPA has become increasingly controversial. It was not renewed by Congress following completion of the Uruguay Round and NAFTA, and President William J. Clinton was rebuffed by Congress in 1997 when he sought new authority. President George W. Bush was able to get TPA through a narrowly divided Congress in 2002, and the authority was used by his administration to win approval of seven bilateral trade agreements, as well as the regional CAFTA. That burst of negotiations underscored the value of TPA in allowing the president to pursue a more ambitious trade policy. But TPA lapsed again in 2007 and has not been renewed since.

Perhaps more significantly, Congress in 2008 rebuffed efforts by the Bush administration to submit a trade agreement with Colombia for approval under TPA, even though the deal had been negotiated under TPA authority. Unable to win assent from the House Democratic leadership, the administration sent the agreement to Capitol Hill regardless, and the leadership responded with a rules change that denied the normal expedited procedures to the Colombia FTA.[90]

That action exposed the fragility of TPA. In essence, TPA amounts to a good-faith promise by Congress to consider trade agreements under special procedural rules. But in reality those rules remain subject to change by Congress at any time. Further, following the reluctance of Congress to move ahead on the agreements with Colombia, Panama, and South Korea under the agreed TPA procedures, the Obama administration entered into negotiations with the three governments to amend and modify the agreements reached under the Bush administration. In practice, the very thing that TPA was intended to prevent—the renegotiation of concluded trade agreements as a result of congressional action or inaction—has played out with all three agreements.

TPA is fundamentally a political compact between the executive branch and Congress to cooperate in advancing trade liberalization. It is not a procedural guarantee.[91] It will be difficult to renew in the absence of broader political agreement on the goals of U.S. trade policy, and even if it could be renewed, there is no guarantee that a future Congress will be bound by the TPA procedures, even for agreements negotiated under that authority.

The periodic reauthorization and lapsing of TPA has created at least three problems for U.S. trade policy. First, the existence or absence of trade-negotiating authority has become a kind of international litmus test for U.S. commitment to trade liberalization. In the absence of congressional authority, it becomes easier for other countries to avoid serious negotiations with the United States, having only to point to the lack of U.S. trade authority as an excuse for avoiding serious engagement.

Second, the renewal of TPA has become a lightning rod for the most ideologically polarized domestic debates over trade. Lael Brainard and Hal Shapiro have rightly called it "the Moby Dick of American trade politics."[92] Under ordinary circumstances, even the most committed of free traders would acknowledge that opening trade has not been equally beneficial for all Americans. And the most passionate trade skeptic would acknowledge that some companies and workers benefit from greater market opportunities abroad even as others are hurt by import competition. When Congress votes on individual trade agreements, these are the sorts of trade-offs that weigh into the final votes. But the renewal of TPA forces each camp into an abstract discussion of the overall costs and benefits of trade, exacerbating, rather than tempering, ideological differences.

Third, in an effort to balance legitimate congressional equities with the broad grant of presidential authority given by TPA, Congress has become increasingly prescriptive, producing long lists of hurdles the administration must jump before a negotiation can be concluded. One of the results has been to reinforce the tendency of the United States to pick as its negotiating partners only small countries that are willing to accept in the negotiations most or all of the congressional parameters.

Recommendations

The United States needs more ambitious and effective trade and investment policies and a more robust enforcement regime as part of a strategy to reestablish strong, broad-based U.S. economic growth in a global economy that has both more opportunities and greater competition than at any time in history. The primary goal of these policies should be to make the United States a more attractive location for the production of world-competitive goods and services.

Better trade and investment policies are only one part of the necessary response to the broader competitive challenge the United States faces, which is going to require a sustained national effort along multiple fronts. These include improvements in education, investment in infrastructure and research, and policy reforms in areas such as taxation and immigration.

The Task Force believes that the primary reason for waning congressional and popular support for U.S. trade policy is that growing global trade and investment—for all the benefits they have brought in terms of lowering consumer prices, improving productivity, and advancing U.S. values and foreign policy goals—have done too little to deliver broad-based job and income growth to Americans.

The Task Force therefore recommends a trade and investment strategy based on seven pillars:

– An ambitious trade negotiations agenda aimed at opening markets for the most competitive U.S.-produced goods and services, especially in the biggest and fastest-growing emerging markets
– A National Investment Initiative that would be the new umbrella for policies on inward and outbound investment that encourage the location of higher-wage production and service jobs in the United States
– A more robust and strategic trade enforcement effort, with the U.S. government playing a more proactive role in ensuring that

U.S. companies and workers are not harmed by trade agreement violations

- Greater efforts to promote exports through more competitive export financing and a more active government role in supporting U.S. overseas sales
- Expanded use of trade to foster development in the world's poorest countries
- A comprehensive worker adjustment and retraining policy
- A new deal with Congress to give the president authority to negotiate trade-opening agreements

A TRADE NEGOTIATING STRATEGY

The United States should refocus its trade negotiating priorities on the sectors and countries that promise the greatest potential gains in terms of new U.S. trade opportunities. These priorities should be expanding services trade, moving beyond the Doha Round, ongoing bilateral and regional negotiations, and revising foreign policy goals.

EXPANDING SERVICES TRADE

The United States should expand market opportunities for U.S. service exports and IPR owners, especially in professional business services that include publishing, software, telecommunications, finance and insurance, real estate, accounting, and engineering.

The original vision of the General Agreement on Trade in Services, a fundamental part of the Uruguay Round agreement, was that it would launch a series of negotiations to achieve progressively greater liberalization in the service sector. The effort, however, has not succeeded in the current Doha Round. The United States must therefore pursue other alternatives with the potential for greater payoff.

The preferable route would be negotiations in the WTO context that built on the progress made in the 1990s on basic telecommunications, financial services, and information technology. Similar plurilateral negotiations that expanded commitments in a variety of service sectors could promise the greatest gains. To be successful, such negotiations would need to include the big developing countries—particularly China and India—that have been reluctant to make deeper commitments.

A second possible route that may be more promising in the near term would be a broader trade agreement covering all the major service sectors that initially involved only the biggest markets. For instance, a services trade agreement between the United States, the EU, Japan, and Canada would set a high standard. It could subsequently be opened to other countries that wish to participate.

The Task Force believes that efforts to open foreign markets for U.S. service industry exports through bilateral and regional negotiations should be a top trade-negotiating priority for the United States.

The U.S. government should also facilitate service exports by working with trading partners to improve international data on services trade, which remains underdeveloped. This includes supporting progress on the OECD's Services Trade Restrictiveness Index and other efforts to better quantify trade protection in services as an aid to negotiations.

MOVING BEYOND THE DOHA ROUND

As the Doha Round negotiations enter their eleventh year with no obvious signs of progress, the issue of what to do about Doha looms particularly large on the trade agenda. Efforts have been made to suggest ways out of the impasse. Some have called for an agreement on a modest package—focused on trade facilitation, reductions in agricultural supports, and additional market opening for the poorest countries—that would put aside more contentious issues for the future. Others have called for setting a firm deadline in an effort to force the difficult compromises necessary to save the round from failure.[93]

Some Task Force members believe that the United States should settle for what is available; others do not believe this is substantively justified or politically viable vis-à-vis Congress. But one way or another, there is consensus in the Task Force that America needs to get beyond the Doha Round and focus on negotiations that offer a bigger prospect of tangible payoffs. Certainly the United States should work toward a deal that includes many of the elements already essentially agreed upon. But the priority should be to define and move forward on a post-Doha trade agenda, for which the WTO must remain central. The U.S.

administration should work with its trading partners to reconfigure the WTO as an ongoing negotiating body.

For instance, the United States would benefit substantially from the expansion of the WTO agreement covering government procurement. Government procurement markets are significant in many large developing countries, where government agencies and state-controlled companies play a much greater role in the economy. The more than forty members and observers of the WTO Government Procurement Agreement (GPA) are currently negotiating the most significant expansion of the agreement in several decades. The United States should also continue to work to bring additional countries—the most important of which is China—into the GPA.

Other issues that could be negotiated under WTO auspices include food and product safety standards, additional liberalization of information, communications, and telecommunications products and services that would build on the landmark 1996 Information Technology Agreement, and the elimination of tariffs and other barriers to trade in environmental goods. Issues on the horizon include the need to set rules for the use of border taxes on carbon or other measures aimed at reducing greenhouse gas emissions. And the increasing scope of WTO dispute settlement decisions, particularly on trade remedy measures, will require negotiations aimed at further clarifying the rules on those issues.

Even agriculture may be ripe for a discrete negotiation. The combination of tight government budgets in the United States and most other advanced economies, and what appears to be a trend toward sustained higher food prices, has the potential to alter significantly the negotiating stances of many countries.[94] Higher prices will increase the willingness of developing countries to cut tariffs on imports to restrain food price inflation. Such tariff reductions would offer increased market access for subsidized U.S. and European farmers, making them more willing to accept additional limitations on domestic subsidies.

One of the bigger challenges in a world of higher prices will be to restrict countries from implementing export restrictions that have the effect of driving up prices for staple crops in other countries. As in other sectors, the changing nature of the agricultural market argues for having an ongoing negotiating process in the WTO that can address new global trade challenges as they arise.

BILATERAL AND REGIONAL NEGOTIATIONS

Alongside continued multilateral efforts, the Task Force believes the United States should pursue tariff-cutting negotiations in the markets with the biggest potential for U.S. exports, such as India and Brazil. These countries are being courted aggressively by major U.S. competitors like the EU and China, and the United States cannot afford to cede these markets.

Certainly such negotiations would not be easy. These countries have been reluctant to cut tariffs more deeply in the Doha Round negotiations. In many cases, however, their concern is less with competition from the United States than from China and other emerging markets, and bilateral negotiations may be easier to conclude. Other issues would arise. Brazil would want increased openings for agricultural exports, including sugar, ethanol, cotton, and orange juice. India would want the United States to address difficult issues of temporary labor mobility and to open opportunities for Indian service companies in the U.S. market.

Such negotiations would likely require the United States to move off its gold standard for trade agreements and be prepared to accept arrangements that fall short of this ideal in one or more of the areas under negotiation. But the potential gains from opening new opportunities in these and other large emerging markets are worth the price of a more flexible U.S. approach.

The United States should also pursue broader regional agreements in Asia and Latin America. The Trans-Pacific Partnership, which is the top negotiating priority for the Obama administration, is an extremely promising initiative. Although the talks are still in their early stages, the TPP could emerge as the vehicle for more comprehensive trade liberalization in the Asia-Pacific region. It also offers an opportunity to begin to harmonize the complex rules of origin in bilateral FTAs and to tackle difficult issues such as appropriate constraints on state-owned enterprises.

With the United States hosting the APEC summit in Hawaii in November 2011, this year offers a particularly good opportunity to continue strengthening U.S. trade ties with the region. Asia is the fastest-growing economic region in the world, and it is critical that the United States pursue an ambitious negotiating agenda in that region. The United States should work to bring Japan and other interested regional participants into the negotiations as soon as possible.

The Task Force believes that a similar model should be used to advance a regional trade framework in Latin America. The United States already has trade agreements with eight Latin American countries—the five CAFTA countries along with the Dominican Republic, Chile, and Peru—with the FTAs with Colombia and Panama now awaiting congressional ratification. Those countries could form the core of a new regional trade agreement along the model of the TPP. Negotiations with Brazil could be part of such an initiative, or could proceed alongside it with the goal of eventually building a regional trading area. Such an initiative would send a strong signal of U.S. reengagement with Latin America and would provide an important balance to efforts by China and the EU to expand their own trading links with the region.

FOREIGN POLICY GOALS

Trade negotiations should largely be crafted around potential economic benefits, but they can sometimes be used to advance larger foreign policy goals. The most pressing need in this regard is the Middle East. In 2003, the United States proposed the negotiation of a U.S.-Middle East Free Trade Area, with a 2013 completion date, but the idea was not pursued vigorously. The main accomplishments to date have been bilateral FTAs with Bahrain and Morocco, Saudi Arabia's accession to the WTO, and the negotiation of Trade and Investment Framework Agreements (TIFAs) with a number of countries, including Saudi Arabia, Yemen, Qatar, Kuwait, and Algeria.

Given the vital importance of Middle East prosperity and stability to U.S. security interests, particularly with the current political reform efforts in the region that could lead to greater democracy, the Task Force believes a more active trade agenda with the Middle East would pay significant dividends. Egypt, which in the past has been proposed as an FTA partner, should be a priority in this regard, both because of its economic and political importance in the region and the United States' interest in nurturing Egypt's democratic transition.

A NATIONAL INVESTMENT INITIATIVE

Historically, the United States has never concerned itself in a systematic way with attracting and retaining foreign investment. As the world's

largest market, it was simply assumed that big companies would make
investing in the United States a high priority. That is no longer the case.
Today, given the importance that investment by multinational corporations has historically played in the American economy, especially
in creating higher wage employment, the United States needs to be
acutely attuned to strengthening itself as an investment location. If current trends continue, smaller contributions to the U.S. economy by less
vibrant multinationals are to be expected, translating into less R&D
and investment, fewer exports, and ultimately fewer jobs.

The Task Force recommends that the Obama administration, with
the active support of Congress, launch a National Investment Initiative (NII) that would complement the National Export Initiative. The
NII should set a target for increasing investment in the United States,
both by domestically headquartered multinational companies and by
foreign multinationals. As with the NEI, a variety of policy instruments
should be brought to bear to encourage the location of investment in the
United States.

The National Investment Initiative should involve action on a variety of fronts, including education, development of infrastructure,
encouragement of high-skilled immigration, expanded government
support for R&D, and other initiatives that enhance the United States
as a primary destination for the location of higher-wage employment.
Two issues that stand out in the context of this report are U.S. international tax and trade policies. In addition, there is a set of U.S. policies specific to international investment—national-security reviews
of international acquisitions, overall federal government support for
inward investment, and bilateral investment treaties—where improvements can be made.

One of the most important policy issues shaping international
investment decisions is taxes. The Task Force favors reform of the U.S.
tax system to encourage the location of job-producing investment in the
United States. The reform should be based on three pillars: a reduction
of the statutory corporate tax rate and measures to simplify the U.S.
corporate tax code; the adoption of a territorial tax system that would
eliminate taxation of foreign-affiliate income of U.S.-based multinationals, bringing the United States in line with other G7 countries; and
serious consideration of adopting a value-added tax to improve the
competitive position of U.S.-based production. The Task Force recognizes the political difficulty of this last pillar, but the international

competitive benefits may be so significant that a VAT should be part of any serious discussion on tax reform.

Fundamental reform of U.S. corporate taxation would raise a number of important practical issues that would need to be addressed to ensure fairness (for example, a transition to territorial taxation would require clearly articulated and enforced rules on transfer pricing). And although broader fiscal reform is beyond the scope of this Task Force, changes to corporate taxation would likely need to be part of a broader solution to the fiscal crisis facing the United States. Despite these challenges, the Task Force believes that making the United States' corporate tax system more competitive should be a top priority of policymakers to support hiring and investment by multinational firms.

Regulations governing cross-border mergers and acquisitions (M&A) should also be improved to facilitate investment. M&A is the predominant way in which foreign multinational companies start their U.S. operations, and FDI is an important share of all U.S. M&A activity.[95] In recent years, however, the tone and substance of U.S. policy toward inward FDI has arguably become more protectionist.

Some executives are concerned that the national security reviews of M&A transactions conducted by the Committee on Foreign Investment in the United States (CFIUS) have become more politicized. This perception results largely from the political pressure that in 2005 led the China National Offshore Oil Corporation (CNOOC) to withdraw its bid for Unocal, and in 2006 caused Dubai Ports World to halt its planned acquisition of some U.S. port facilities. Reviews to the CFIUS process in the wake of those incidents have improved the process in some ways, though many proposed deals are undergoing longer, in-depth inspections by CFIUS that add to the cost and uncertainty for foreign buyers.

The issue is particularly difficult with respect to China, which has shown an increased eagerness to make direct investments in the United States rather than to continue building its portfolio holdings. Encouraging Chinese investment is difficult because much of its overseas expansion has been through investments in production of commodities, and the United States is not a primary target for that sort of investment. Certain other sectors in which Chinese companies have global ambitions, such as telecommunications, raise particular national security sensitivities for the United States. State-owned companies also account for more than 80 percent of Chinese outward investment, which raises additional issues.

But, despite the difficulties, encouraging increased Chinese investment should be a top U.S. priority. Hard investments in assets are
inherently more stable than large-scale purchases of liquid assets like
Treasury bills, and are desirable for that reason alone. The history of
the U.S. trade conflict with Japan also showed that increased foreign
investment helps reduce tensions; as Japanese investment expanded in
more states, U.S. politicians acquired a growing stake in maintaining
positive trade relations with Japan. A similar development with China
would be welcome.

Other executives point to the Buy American provisions of the 2009
American Recovery and Reinvestment Act as having sent a negative
message. To offset this, the United States should set a more welcoming
and optimistic tone. A positive step in this direction was the "Statement
by the President on United States Commitment to Open Investment
Policy," issued on June 20, 2011, in which President Obama discussed
the many benefits inward investment has brought to the U.S. economy
and said, "The United States reaffirms our open investment policy, a
commitment to treat all investors in a fair and equitable manner under
the law."

A four-paragraph statement alone, however, is not enough. Greater
efforts should be made at the national level to attract foreign investors.
The United States has never seen encouraging investment as a national
priority; most government initiatives to attract FDI are now carried
out at the state and local levels, and the federal government plays a
smaller supporting role. U.S. investment promotion effectiveness lags
far beyond most other developed countries, and even well behind many
developing countries. In a 2009 review of investment promotion efforts
by the World Bank, the United States was ranked near the bottom of
OECD countries in terms of best practices for attracting foreign investors.[96] With competition for investment increasing across the globe, the
United States must do more to actively market itself as an investment
location.

Finally, the United States should continue negotiating better rules for
facilitating overseas investment, including bilateral investment treaties
(BITs) and strong investment provisions in bilateral and multilateral
trade agreements. The certainty created by investment rules is important not only for U.S. companies seeking to do business abroad, but for
foreign companies seeking to operate in the United States. The United
States has been engaged in a long, difficult, and contentious internal

review of its approach to BIT negotiations, and now it needs to develop and implement a strategy, especially in negotiations with countries with large state-owned sectors.

The Task Force believes that the United States can succeed in attracting additional investment and promoting export growth only in an international economy in which investment is facilitated and safeguarded by mutually negotiated, binding rules. The United States should be a leader in such negotiations.

STRENGTHENING TRADE ENFORCEMENT

The Task Force recommends that the administration and Congress pursue the following measures.

BETTER INTELLIGENCE

The United States needs to gather earlier and better intelligence on the industrial policy practices of foreign governments to identify trends that could be damaging to U.S.-based industry and the American workforce. The current system, because it relies on formal complaints brought by companies or labor unions, means that the U.S. government becomes fully engaged only when considerable harm may already have been done to U.S. economic interests. The USTR's office currently gathers a wealth of detailed information in its annual National Trade Estimate (NTE) Report on Foreign Trade Barriers, as well as in its annual report to Congress on China's compliance with its WTO obligations. The recent ITC report on the impact of Chinese IPR infringements and industrial policies on the U.S. economy is a solid model of the type of empirical work needed to help focus the U.S. trade agenda.

The Task Force believes there is a need for greater sustained, high-level attention to compliance issues within the U.S. government and Congress. In addition to the NTE report, the administration should present to Congress on a regular basis an Enforcement Priority List that identifies the most significant outstanding enforcement problems and its progress in resolving those issues.

Although WTO rules no longer allow for the unilateral sanction threats of the old Section 301 provisions, such identification would give additional attention to foreign trade barriers and raise pressure on the U.S. administration to act through the WTO or other dispute procedures. Such identification of priority problems is done currently for intellectual property issues under the Special 301 procedure, but it should be expanded to cover a broader range of enforcement issues.

MORE PROACTIVE GOVERNMENT ROLE

The U.S. government should become more proactive in initiating WTO cases or pursuing other remedies. The Task Force believes that enforcement needs to become more of a government function and less private sector–led, primarily because the interests of U.S. companies are increasingly conflicted.

Enforcement actions initiated by the government could help shield companies that are being harmed by trade violations but fear retaliation, but the government should be prepared to initiate certain cases even in the face of corporate opposition. Although the majority of trade actions are still likely to be initiated by U.S. companies or labor unions, the U.S. government is responsible for broader U.S. economic interests and should be aggressive in enforcing trade rules that benefit all Americans, regardless of specific private interests.

TRADE REMEDY LAWS

The United States needs to rethink some of its approaches to the use of trade remedy laws. Domestically, some of the companies and workers most in need of trade relief are unable to bring cases because of the cost or the difficulty of organizing a response in fragmented industries. The U.S. government has the power to launch AD/CVD cases on its own authority. This self-initiation power, however, has been allowed to atrophy and has not been used since the early 1990s. It should be revived and used more frequently when the U.S. government believes that companies and workers are being harmed by unfair trade but have been unable to bring their own cases. Where self-initiation is not warranted, the government should at least make certain that small companies are aware of the full range of Commerce Department technical assistance available to help them through the process.

At the same time, the growing use of trade remedy laws in major U.S. export markets requires rethinking the U.S. approach to trade remedy laws in international negotiations. Historically, the United States has insisted on maintaining maximum flexibility to impose trade remedies at home, even at the cost of other negotiating objectives. But as other countries increase their use of such measures, the United States needs to give equal weight to ensuring that U.S. exports are not unreasonably disadvantaged by trade remedies in foreign markets.

The United States needs to more closely integrate its trade defense mechanisms with an offensive strategy of market opening abroad. The history of U.S. trade disputes with more protected economies has demonstrated that import restrictions do little more than buy a bit of breathing room for affected companies but do nothing to change the competitive equation. A strategy needs to be formulated for trade relief not geared solely toward adjustment by U.S. companies and workers, but also to making foreign markets more open to U.S. imports and conditioning U.S. market access on foreign governments living up to their trade obligations. This would require a more active U.S. government approach, rather than a passive stance of waiting for companies or labor unions to bring forward formal complaints.

STATE-OWNED ENTERPRISES
AND INTELLECTUAL PROPERTY PIRACY

The U.S. government should develop a broad strategy for reducing the trade-distorting practices associated with many SOEs or state-backed "national champions," under the principle of promoting competitive neutrality. The goal would be to create and enforce new disciplines that limit the ability of governments to use financial supports and discriminatory regulatory practices to enhance the competitiveness of favored companies. The strategy should include negotiating new rules in U.S. bilateral and regional trade agreements and investment agreements, including the TPP; initiating OECD negotiations on a comprehensive competitive neutrality agreement; and eventually bringing such disciplines to the WTO. The goal should be the broadest possible international agreement restricting anticompetitive behavior by governments that distort competition in global markets.

The United States should also develop new tools for combating intellectual property piracy abroad. The issue has been a high priority for many years, but progress has been frustratingly slow and the costs to the U.S. economy are high and rising. The government could work more closely with U.S. companies, for instance, to discourage sourcing from overseas suppliers that are major users of pirated software.

WTO DISPUTE SETTLEMENT

The United States should work to streamline the WTO dispute settlement process. The average dispute case before the WTO takes nearly two years to complete. Although in many cases lengthy analyses are unavoidable, the United States should engage with other WTO members to find ways to accelerate the process.

The United States needs to encourage the revitalization of a WTO negotiating process for dealing with enforcement issues. As the WTO dispute system comes to operate more and more like a court process, the decisions are revealing serious issues with elements of the WTO agreements that need to be resolved through negotiations. If the core WTO agreements cannot in practice be amended, enforcement of trade commitments is likely to grow more difficult over time.

BILATERAL NEGOTIATIONS

The United States should reinvigorate the bilateral negotiating process with countries other than China. High-level engagement with the EU, Canada, Mexico, and Japan would help bring sustained attention to important trade, investment, and regulatory issues.[97] The recently announced U.S.-Brazil Commission on Economic and Trade Relations was a positive step in this regard.

CURRENCY

That an undervalued currency can create competitive disadvantages for countries saddled with strong currencies is not in question. The issue for this Task Force was whether trade tools would provide an effective remedy for countries that intervene to artificially depress the value of their currencies to gain export advantage.

China is the most important country for the United States in this regard. It is not clear, however, that trade instruments are useful in pressing China to accelerate its gradual and intermittent revaluation of the renminbi. It is unclear, for instance, that the United States would prevail in a WTO challenge against China's currency regime, and a loss at the WTO would further reduce U.S. ability to influence China positively on other issues. Even a win before the WTO would take many years to work through the appeals process, and China could easily drag its heels on compliance. Congressional legislation that truly punished China through tariff measures could violate WTO rules. More narrowly targeted legislation that allows currency misalignment to be considered a de facto export subsidy in trade remedy cases would have limited impact, and might still run afoul of the WTO rules.

The issue of currency valuations, along with broader structural imbalances, is more likely to get a positive response as part of a series of coordinated actions by several countries. Greater progress is likely possible by working through the International Monetary Fund (IMF) or the G20. The United States should also continue working closely with other countries, such as Brazil, that have been hurt by currency manipulation.

Finally, the United States needs to do more to strengthen the dispute settlement system by complying promptly and fully with adverse WTO rulings and other trade decisions. The U.S. record on compliance is reasonably good, but in several disputes the United States was extremely slow in coming into compliance with WTO decisions. If the United States is to push successfully for better compliance with trade agreements, it must lead by example.

PROMOTING TRADE COMPETITIVENESS

The Task Force believes that the United States needs a strategic plan for increasing overseas markets for the export of U.S.-produced goods and services. The government needs to play a more active role in assessing foreign market opportunities, identifying priorities among products and services, and carrying out a long-term plan to bolster U.S. performance in world markets. This will involve close coordination with the private sector, which possesses most of the information needed to engage in this effort.

The United States has been a laggard in export promotion efforts and has much to learn from countries like Germany, France, Japan, and Canada in this regard. The Task Force recommends that the Obama administration immediately launch an in-depth study, to be completed

within ninety days, of the tools used by countries whose export promotion programs have been more successful than those of the United
States. With appropriate modifications for the particular circumstances
of the United States, this study should set benchmarks for best practices
that would guide future U.S. efforts.

The administration and Congress should support expansion of
lending by the Export-Import Bank. Trade financing is critical to helping U.S. companies secure contracts in many parts of the world, and
U.S. support remains well behind that of most major competitors. Two
priorities should be the expansion of overall lending and a concerted
effort to discourage financing by emerging market countries that does
not meet the requirements of the OECD Export Credit Arrangement.
The Ex-Im Bank has demonstrated an increased willingness to match
financing offers by other export credit agencies that tie credit terms to
foreign aid or otherwise do not comply with the OECD terms.[98]

The Ex-Im Bank should continue to be aggressive on this front, and
the administration should work with other OECD countries to press
China and other outlying countries to accede to the OECD arrangement. Further, the bank should eliminate its statutory 85 percent domestic content requirement and instead deal with projects on a case-by-case
basis with the goal of ensuring maximum benefits for the American
workforce from any supported contracts. Similarly, Congress should
eliminate the outdated requirement that Ex-Im-backed exports be
transported only in U.S. vessels, a restriction that unnecessarily raises
costs for U.S. exporters.

The efforts of U.S. competitors, most notably Germany, dwarf
those of the U.S. government, creating a competitive disadvantage for
the United States that can be offset only by a more active government
role. The administration should continue to expand its efforts under the
National Export Initiative to make export promotion a top priority for
the government, including intervention by senior government officials
when appropriate.

In addition, a case is also to be made for broader targeted government support in certain critical industries. The notion of the government "picking winners and losers" immediately generates controversy,
but some industries are particularly important for U.S. national security
and trade competitiveness. In the 1980s, for instance, the emerging U.S.
semiconductor industry faced competition from Asia that threatened
to drive many U.S. producers out of business. The U.S. government
responded with an array of measures, including trade enforcement and

direct support to the industry through government-financed research and development and easing of antitrust restrictions.

Today the U.S. semiconductor industry is the second-largest U.S. exporting industry, holds a near 50 percent share of the world market, and continues to be the world's technological leader. Yet the U.S. lead is still challenged as governments in other countries shower incentives designed to encourage location of advanced fabrication facilities.[99]

A similar case could be made today for greater targeted support for clean energy initiatives. Reducing the use of conventional energy should be among the highest U.S. priorities, for both national security and environmental reasons. Yet though the United States made more than 40 percent of the world's solar cells in the mid-1990s, for instance, today it manufactures only 7 percent. China has invested heavily in promoting its domestic production of wind, solar, biomass, and other renewable energy technologies. Although driven largely by domestic energy needs, China has also used an array of incentives to promote development and export of clean energy technologies. These include export restrictions on rare earth minerals, government subsidies, and discriminatory treatment of imports. One result has been to reduce sharply U.S. exports to China of clean energy goods and to displace U.S. exports in third markets such as Europe. China earlier this year agreed to remove some of its subsidies, on wind power, in response to a WTO action brought by the United States after a Section 301 complaint filed by the United Steelworkers union.

Surveys of investors indicate that government political and regulatory support is critical for attracting private investment to the industry in the United States rather than encouraging clean energy investors to pursue opportunities overseas.[100] There are many difficult questions in terms of how such support programs should be designed and implemented, but the strategic interest in building a vibrant U.S. clean energy industry argues for a more active government role in promoting this sector.

TRADE AND DEVELOPMENT

Congress should move quickly to reauthorize the trade preferences programs that have been allowed to lapse, the GSP and the ATPA. In addition, the United States should offer more ambitious and stable trade preferences to the world's poorest countries.

The Task Force favors immediate expansion of existing U.S. trade preference programs to provide additional help to the poorest countries, particularly in sub-Saharan Africa. The United States should offer duty-free and quota-free treatment for all imports from these countries, which would fulfill a long-standing commitment.

The United States and other advanced economies have agreed as part of the Millennium Development Goals to provide duty-free and quota-free access for imports from the world's poorest countries. That commitment was reiterated at the 2005 WTO ministerial meeting in Hong Kong. Because these countries account for less than 1 percent of U.S. imports, the impact on domestic producers would be negligible, and such a program would not significantly erode the preference that the United States gives to other countries.[101] The United States should also encourage other countries, especially the more successful emerging markets, to offer similar treatment for imports from the poorest countries.

The United States should also offer incentives for countries to move beyond the current preference arrangements. U.S. preference programs have been constructed on the notion that the poorest countries should not be required to open their markets to imports as a condition to receiving tariff-free treatment for their products. Although this approach makes sense, it is also true that many of these countries would benefit by opening their markets more fully to imports. Competitive imports can help raise productivity across the economy, not just in the export-oriented sectors favored under preference programs. The Task Force believes the United States should create additional incentives in its preference programs to encourage developing countries to open their markets to U.S. goods on a reciprocal basis.

The United States should extend duty-free and quota-free treatment on a permanent basis to such countries, provided the other conditions of eligibility continue to be met. This would create an incentive for countries to agree to further trade liberalization but would not require the extensive and detailed negotiations involved in bilateral free trade agreements.

Similarly, much as a single template for bilateral trade agreements is unlikely to work for deals with the biggest emerging markets, greater flexibility is also needed in dealing with the poorest countries. The EU has negotiated so-called Economic Partnership Agreements (EPAs) in Africa, for example, which fall well short of U.S.-standard FTAs but are a step beyond purely preferential arrangements. Under the EPAs, European companies will enjoy preferences in Africa not available to U.S. companies. The United States should pursue similar arrangements with willing developing countries.

Finally, the United States could make a major contribution to development by cutting sharply its subsidies to U.S. farmers and pressing the EU and other major agricultural producers to do the same. This would open new export opportunities for developing-country farms. Subsidy cuts make sense for a host of other reasons, including rising food prices and the burgeoning fiscal deficits facing the United States and many other countries.

COMPREHENSIVE ADJUSTMENT ASSISTANCE

The United States needs a set of expanded, integrated policies that fundamentally reshape U.S. labor-market policy. Congressional funding for TAA expired in February 2011. Although TAA should be renewed, the United States needs to establish a broader set of benefits for workers that would combine the best elements of unemployment insurance, TAA, and training programs authorized by the Workforce Investment Act (WIA) with a single integrated approach to adjustment and training designed to return individuals to the workforce as quickly as possible.

The merits of an integrated approach to adjustment and training are twofold. A better integrated adjustment program would help the unemployed return to the workforce with skills capable of ensuring continuing employment. And cost savings would flow from eliminating separate qualifications and administrative staff for the multiple programs that currently exist.

A broader safety net for American workers should include a wage-loss insurance program for older workers to supplement their income when they take employment at a lower-paying job. Wage-loss insurance can reduce the risk associated with workers specializing in particular occupations, and it can also benefit society by encouraging workers to take riskier but higher-output jobs that pay higher wages without the fear of a significant income decline in the event of a job loss.

An expanded safety net for unemployed U.S. workers would need to be financed. The Task Force acknowledges that any proposal to expand federal spending is challenging in the current fiscal environment. But the cost of stronger labor-market supports must be set against the cost of the drift in U.S. policy away from trade and investment liberalization. The cost of not expanding public support for American workers will likely be continued weak public support for international trade and, in turn, less global engagement and lower national income.

TRADE NEGOTIATING AUTHORITY

The Task Force believes that a grant of special congressional negotiating authority remains essential if the United States is to pursue an ambitious and effective trade policy. Modern trade agreements are generally too complicated to be dealt with under normal legislative rules, and the diplomatic consequences of a congressional refusal to act on negotiated trade deals can be significant.

What are the future options for renewing negotiating authority? One possibility would be for the administration to seek a congressional vote to make the president's authority to negotiate trade agreements permanent. Some members of the Task Force favor this option. A permanent grant of negotiating authority would establish the assumption once and for all that the president enjoys the authority to negotiate trade agreements, subject to ratification by Congress. Legislators' authority could be protected by requiring that a specific congressional resolution be approved to grant fast track procedures to a particular negotiation or set of negotiations, preferably at the onset. The resolution would be an opportunity for Congress to authorize or reject a particular negotiation and to set specific parameters.[102]

Pursuing such a permanent grant of authority in the current political climate presents two difficulties, however. First, such a proposal would almost certainly trigger an all-out ideological struggle over U.S. trade policy in Congress, exacerbating and hardening political divisions on trade that are already deeply entrenched. It would likely draw opposition not just from those skeptical about trade, but from members of Congress worried about giving a blank check to the administration. Second, as the experiences with the South Korea, Colombia, and Panama FTAs have demonstrated, even a permanent grant of authority would be no guarantee that a future Congress would feel bound by those rules.

Therefore, the Task Force recommends that, while retaining permanent trade negotiating authority as a long-term objective, the Obama administration and Congress should adopt a more flexible and prag-matic approach to the issue of trade negotiating authority.

What this would mean in practice is that the president should ask Congress for TPA only in the context of specific proposed agreements, and only for those where TPA is necessary. Some trade agreements are certainly possible without invoking TPA; Congress approved the U.S.-Jordan Free Trade Agreement in 2001, for example, under normal congressional procedures. For smaller agreements in particu-lar, where the changes to U.S. laws are modest, the risk of Congress's approving damaging amendments to a completed trade agreement is likely to be small.

For ambitious agreements under the WTO, for broader regional agreements like the pending TPP, and for large bilateral deals, the administration would need to ask Congress for a specific grant of nego-tiating authority. Such a request could seek authority to conclude mul-tiple negotiations. There should be no illusion that such requests would always be readily accepted by Congress, but this would have benefits as well as costs. It would allow the debate to be focused earlier on the concrete issues of whether a particular trade agreement or agreements would be in the interest of the United States, rather than on the more abstract question of whether trade liberalization in general is beneficial. If Congress does not see the merits in a particular negotiation, it could reject the proposal up front rather than block agreements already nego-tiated, which is damaging to U.S. credibility and can harm diplomatic relations and broader security interests.

Over time, if a pattern of cooperation between the executive and congressional branches on trade can be rebuilt, then permanent trade negotiating authority along the lines discussed would be desirable and should be pursued. But no procedural mechanism can overcome the central problem, which is the need to rebuild a stronger national con-sensus over the proper direction for trade policy. Whatever legislative procedures are adopted should encourage cooperation rather than exacerbate divisions.

Conclusion

The expansion of trade and international investment over the past half century has contributed enormously to poverty reduction, to improved living standards, and to more peaceful and stable international politics. This was accomplished in no small part because of the leading role played by the United States and its allies in developing, negotiating, and implementing global and regional trading rules that facilitate commerce.

That leadership has waned in recent years because of deep domestic political divisions over trade policy that arise largely from the very real economic difficulties too many Americans face. The United States needs to develop and implement a set of trade and investment policies that do more to bring the gains from global commerce to a greater number of Americans.

The Task Force does not underestimate the scale of this challenge. Better trade and investment policies are only one part of a larger series of measures needed to enhance the ability of Americans to prosper in an increasingly competitive global economy. And even as the United States works to address these challenges, its competitors will not be standing still.

The United States, however, enjoys many advantages—a diverse, educated workforce, the best universities, the most innovative companies, and the world's largest consumer market. The task is to use trade and investment policies more effectively to leverage those advantages to the benefit of the American people while expanding and strengthening trade rules that have brought great benefits to much of the world.

America's future prosperity lies in becoming a more successful trading nation, and the measures this Task Force recommends are critical to securing that future.

Additional and Dissenting Views

As the report notes, trade policy should largely reflect potential economic benefits but can sometimes be crafted to support foreign policy and global development goals as well. The report argues for improved trade relations with Egypt and other countries in the Middle East as one example. A similar case can be made for Pakistan. Pakistan currently faces high tariffs, particularly on its textile and apparel exports; duty-free, quota-free access to the U.S. market would contribute to a more secure environment there and help create jobs—both very much in the U.S. interest. A report of the Center for Global Development makes the foreign policy and development case for unilateral extension of that benefit; a related research study indicates that the expected additional imports would have virtually no impact on U.S. production.

The report also argues well the logic of the United States continuing its long-standing leadership in developing and adhering to fair rules of the game, even when in the short run it is not in the interest of every U.S. firm. For developing countries, there are two issues where the United States might recover some of its leadership if the difficult domestic politics can be managed. One is tobacco: the United States should make it a matter of official U.S. trade policy to refrain from seeking tobacco tariff reductions and exclude tobacco-related investments from future free trade and bilateral investment treaties with developing countries. Another is capital controls: in any future bilateral trade agreements with developing countries, the United States ought to recognize, as has the International Monetary Fund, that complete and immediate opening of capital markets is not necessarily in the interest of all countries all the time.

Nancy Birdsall
joined by James W. Owens and Laura D'Andrea Tyson

I wholeheartedly support the overall Task Force proposal that we "adopt a pro-American trade policy that brings to more Americans more of the benefits of global engagement." But I must disagree with many of the specific policy recommendations because they would only serve to reinforce, deepen, and extend an approach to globalization that empowers private capital and restricts the ability of government to promote the general welfare. That singular focus has contributed significantly to the dire economic and social circumstances the United States finds itself in today. It has benefited corporate interests at the expense of working Americans. I therefore cannot support the report.

It is, however, noteworthy and important that the report acknowledges that this period of trade liberalization has not done enough in bringing economic benefits to U.S. workers. Working Americans have experienced this and it accounts for their skepticism about the value of the global economy. Today, we are experiencing high levels of unemployment and underemployment. Wages remain stagnant. Communities have been devastated as manufacturing plants have closed to move production offshore. Yet corporate executive salaries are soaring, and income distribution is more skewed than at any time since the Gilded Age. The rich are getting richer, and the poor, poorer. We need to chart a new course.

The Task Force report is truly ambitious and space prevents comments on all its recommendations. While I support calls for a stronger governmental role in addressing unfair and harmful trade practices, and the need for comprehensive worker adjustment programs, I am concerned that two major recommendations—an enlarged trade and investment liberalization negotiating agenda, and a reduction in corporate taxes—will only repeat the mistakes of the past.

Before embarking on more free trade agreements, the United States needs to better define its national interest. Simply saying that we should focus on increasing exports will not make it so. Indeed, past negotiations have facilitated the outsourcing of production rather than increases in exports. As the report notes in part, U.S. multinational corporations, over the last decade, cut 2.9 million jobs at home while adding 2.4 million offshore. And much of that overseas production was exported back to America, devastating domestic manufacturing.

While it is clear that the tax structure is in need of reform, simply reducing corporate taxes in the hope of securing more investment is misguided. Today, corporate profits are at record levels, U.S. companies pay less in taxes as a percent of GDP than ever, and by that measure are lower than most other OECD countries. Corporations should pay their fair share, not less.

Trade and investment liberalization has caused America to become the world's largest debtor nation. It is this imbalance that has been harmful to U.S. workers and threatens the global trading system. Addressing this imbalance needs to be in the forefront of any policy approach. In short, we need to produce more of what we consume. Simple belief in the so-called free market and hopes for the best are not sufficient.

Leo W. Gerard*

In the "Comprehensive Adjustment Assistance" section of the report, the Task Force calls on the United States "to establish a broader set of benefits for workers." I am concerned about the cost and affordability of the broadened assistance that the Task Force suggests, particularly the costs associated with a wage-loss insurance program for older workers.

Trent Lott
joined by William M. Thomas

This report is a huge contribution to the debate on the role of trade and its effects on American workers. I am not as convinced as much as others on the extent of the past benefits of trade for our country, and also do believe that a pro-American trade policy should, under strategic or other appropriate circumstances, include a "Buy American" or, more appropriately, a "Made in the USA" initiative. America needs a new plan for a twenty-first-century economy, and this report offers important considerations in the role of trade in America's future.

Andrew L. Stern

China is the third-largest and fastest-growing market for U.S. exports in a wide range of products. China also receives a major share of the foreign direct investment of U.S. multinational companies. Access to China's market is a significant factor in the success of many U.S.

*Gerard participated in the Task Force but did not endorse the general thrust of the report.

companies. Many of the practices that impede access to China's market and many of the promotional policies that play a prominent role in China's development strategy are either inadequately covered or are difficult to enforce by the WTO. These practices include indigenous innovation policies, preferential procurement policies (China is not a signatory to the WTO Government Procurement Agreement), national standards that favor national champions, lax enforcement of intellectual property protection, and implicit or explicit local content rules in strategic sectors like renewable energy. The United States should continue to treat market access barriers as a priority issue in its bilateral strategic dialogue with China, should lodge WTO cases against such barriers when they violate China's WTO commitments, and should encourage China's other trading partners to challenge such barriers in regional and multilateral negotiations.

Laura D'Andrea Tyson

The theory of international trade recognizes that the benefits of trade are not evenly distributed—there are winners and losers. Exports create high-wage jobs and enrich communities for some Americans, but imports destroy jobs and impoverish communities for others. Workers who lose their jobs often suffer prolonged periods of joblessness, lose access to health care, and earn substantially lower wages when they find new jobs. But theory also predicts that the economy-wide gains from trade outweigh the dislocation costs of lost jobs and wages. Evidence confirms this prediction—at least so far. Given the large net gains from trade, the United States could afford to compensate workers and communities for their trade-related losses. But the U.S. safety net is full of holes, and compensation to offset such losses is marginal. And now there are reasons to fear that these losses are getting larger and affecting a larger fraction of American workers.

As China and other emerging-market economies have opened their markets, the global supply of available labor has soared. According to the International Monetary Fund, the global labor supply has risen fourfold since 1980. Most of the new global workers are unskilled, with secondary-school educations or lower, but even the global supply of college graduates has increased by 50 percent. The results of these changes are easy to predict: downward pressure on the wages of workers in the United States and other advanced industrial countries, and an increase in the returns to capital and to individuals with specialized skills that are in limited global supply. A growing number of U.S. workers is now competing for jobs with cheaper foreign workers and facing lower wages, lost jobs, and greater job insecurity. According to Paul Krugman, it is hard to avoid the conclusion that growing U.S. trade with emerging market countries is reducing the real wages of many workers and perhaps most workers in the United States.

During the last two decades, job opportunities in the United States have polarized, with expanding opportunities in both high-skill, high-wage jobs and low-skill, low-wage jobs coupled with contracting opportunities in middle-wage, middle-skill white-collar and blue-collar jobs. Research indicates that there are two key contributors to the polarization of the U.S. labor market: the automation of routine work, and the international integration of labor markets through trade, and more recently through offshoring. Most economists believe that the former is more important than the latter, but there is no definite empirical evidence on this point because both factors often go together. The bottom line is that both technology and trade are adversely affecting middle-skill, middle-wage jobs and contributing to wage stagnation for the median worker and increasing income inequality.

Laura D'Andrea Tyson

I endorse the recommendations in this report and believe the descriptive parts of the report to be generally fair and accurate. However, I do not share the report's view that trade policy in Washington is stymied because public support for these policies has declined. Public attitudes toward trade have always been complicated. There was not clear public support for trade liberalization in the 1980s. There was not clear support for trade liberalization in the 1990s.

The public does not come together to celebrate the passage of trade agreements. But it does not come together to oppose them either. There were no marches on Washington after passage of the Bush-era trade agreements. Most people outside Washington pay little attention to these matters. Special interests, however, do pay close attention. It is the power of these interests that explains the inability to move forward with a trade agenda. Suggesting that trade policy is stymied because of public attitudes outside Washington have changed is misleading. The growing hostility to trade policy is a Washington phenomenon.

To be clear, I do not deny that a growing number of Americans are wondering whether America is in decline and whether their children will have good jobs. The country has serious challenges. We need to do more to enhance our competitiveness and address growing income inequality, including improving education, reducing regulatory burdens, and curbing health-care costs.

Blaming America's problems on trade policy may seem politically expedient, but it is shortsighted. In the long run, this expediency backfires. Public attitudes toward Congress have deteriorated, in my humble opinion, because they see a political class that is more interested in sideshows than in solving problems in common sense ways. The trade agenda has been caught in this *Alice in Wonderland* landscape.

There is often a yawning gap between what Americans see as sensible and relevant issues and what Washington debates. The U.S.-Colombia trade agreement has languished without passage for four years. Yet virtually any American stopped on the street of their home town and asked, "Would you support a bill that provides U.S. exporters with the same access to Colombia that we already provide here to their exporters?" would say, "Of course." For some reason, this common sense public attitude cannot penetrate the Beltway.

Public attitudes toward trade are mixed. They always have been. What is clear, however, is that exit polls consistently show that a candidate's trade policy barely registers when voters cast their ballots. For this reason, I am not convinced that the stymied trade agenda is due to changing attitudes in the country.

John K. Veroneau

There is no acceptable substitute for the United States exercising leadership in shaping the international economic environment to foster its interests. There is no pause on the part of other countries pursuing what they see as their own trade interests. Bilateral and regional arrangements excluding the United States are proliferating. Inaction by the United States in proposing international trade initiatives has adverse consequences. It can only lead to U.S. goods and services receiving less favorable treatment than that accorded to competitors from other countries.

Realistically, the United States is not going to close its market; the primary challenge for U.S. trade policy is maintaining and further opening of foreign markets. Success in gaining benefits from trade agreements, past and present, depends most heavily on domestic policies—creating the conditions for America remaining a primary location for innovation—which includes not only invention but production. This report clearly builds on a foundation of domestic policies that foster American economic strength, including the creation of good jobs in sufficient quantity.

The thrust of American policies after the Second World War has been to define its own interests broadly as fostering global economic growth. Trade agreements today must address additional common interests—access to food to enhance food security, access to critical raw materials to avoid dislocations of supply, assuring food and product safety in a manner that does not constitute protectionism, adding disciplines for state-owned and state-supported enterprises that compete with private companies, creating free trade in environmental goods and services, and similarly improving access to information and information and communications technology goods and services, among a substantial list of priorities.

This CFR report, taking into account the concerns raised in the comments in these appended pages, should form the basis for crafting an action plan that is bipartisan, to be formulated by the administration with full congressional support.

Alan Wm. Wolff

Endnotes

1. Pew Global Attitudes Project poll, June 17, 2010, http://pewglobal.org/2010/06/17/obama-more-popular-abroad-than-at-home/4/#chapter-3-economic-issues. See also Bruce Stokes, "Public Support for Trade Policy," Working Paper, Transatlantic Task Force on Trade, German Marshall Fund, July 2011.

2. Jeffrey M. Jones, "Americans More Negative Than Positive About Foreign Trade: Have Held More Negative Views Since 2005," Gallup World Affairs poll, February 18, 2009.

3. Martin Wolf, "In the Grip of a Great Convergence," *Financial Times*, January 4, 2011.

4. David Riker, "Do Jobs in Export Industries Still Pay More?" U.S. Commerce Department, Office of Competition and Economic Analysis, July 2010, http://www.trade.gov/mas/ian/build/groups/public/@tg_ian/documents/webcontent/tg_ian_003062.pdf.

5. John Tschetter, "Exports Support American Jobs," U.S. Department of Commerce, International Trade Administration, March 2010, http://www.trade.gov/publications/pdfs/exports-support-american-jobs.pdf.

6. Michael Spence and Sandile Hlatshwayo, "The Evolving Structure of the American Economy and the Employment Challenge," Working Paper, Council on Foreign Relations Press, March 2011.

7. The McKinsey Global Institute recently produced a detailed set of employment forecasts for the U.S. economy and concluded that only with very high levels of job creation—some twenty-one million jobs in the next nine years—would the United States be able to return to full employment by 2020. Among the report's recommendations was that the United States must "harness globalization to create more U.S. jobs" by attracting foreign investment and encouraging exports. See James Manyika, Susan Lund, Byron Auguste, Lenny Mendonca, Tim Welsh, and Sreevivas Ramaswamy, "An economy that works: Job creation and America's future," June 2011, http://www.mckinsey.com/mgi/publications/us_jobs/pdfs/MGI_us_jobs_full_report.pdf.

8. Yuqing Xing and Neal Detert, "How the iPhone Widens the United States Trade Deficit with the People's Republic of China," ADBI Working Paper Series, December 2010.

9. Shimelse Ali and Uri Dadush, "Trade in intermediates and economic policy," VOX, February 9, 2011, http://www.voxeu.org.

10. Pascal Lamy, "As trade changes rapidly, you must help guide WTO, Lamy tells global business," speech, May 12, 2011, http://www.wto.org.

11. "World trade statisticians set up plans to improve trade figures," International Trade Statistics, February 7, 2011, http://www.wto.org.

12. "Prepared Remarks for Under Secretary of Commerce for International Trade Francisco Sanchez," U.S. Department of Commerce, September 14, 2010.

13. John Ward, "The Services Sector: How Best to Measure It?" International Trade Commission, September 2010, http://www.trade.gov; see also *International Flows of Invisibles: Trade in Services and Intangibles in the Era of Globalization*, Marshall B. Reinsdorf and Matthew J. Slaughter, eds., CRIW-NBER Conference Volume (Chicago: University of Chicago Press, 2009.)

14. The Council on Foreign Relations is working to address many of these issues through its Renewing America initiative. Visa and immigration issues were also addressed by CFR in the 2009 Independent Task Force report *U.S. Immigration Policy*, chaired by Jeb Bush and Thomas F. McLarty, and education issues will be addressed in a forthcoming Independent Task Force on U.S. Education Reform and National Security, chaired by Joel I. Klein and Condoleezza Rice.

15. See Edward Gresser, "Labor and Environment in Trade Since NAFTA: Activists Have Achieved Less, and More, Than They Realize," *Wake Forest Law Review*, vol. 45, 2011.

16. I. M. Destler, *American Trade Politics*, 4th ed., p. 331.

17. Office of the United States Trade Representative (OUSTR), "The 2008 Trade Policy Agenda and 2007 Annual Report," p.3, http://www.ustr.gov/sites/default/files/uploads/reports/2008/asset_upload_file273_14560.pdf.

18. OUSTR, "The 2009 Trade Policy Agenda and 2008 Annual Report," p. 1, http://www.ustr.gov/about-us/press-office/reports-and-publications/2009/2009-trade-policy-agenda-and-2008-annual-report.

19. OUSTR, "The 2010 Trade Policy Agenda and 2009 Annual Report," p. 2, http://www.ustr.gov/2010-trade-policy-agenda.

20. *Report to the President on the National Export Initiative: The Export Promotion Cabinet's Plan for Doubling U.S. Exports in Five Years*, September 2010, http://www.whitehouse.gov/sites/default/files/nei_report_9-16-10_full.pdf.

21. For a summary of these estimates and studies, see Grant D. Aldonas, Robert Z. Lawrence, and Matthew J. Slaughter, "Succeeding in the Global Economy: A New Policy Agenda for the American Worker," Financial Services Forum policy research report, June 2007.

22. *Building Support for More Open Trade*, report of an Independent Task Force (New York: Council on Foreign Relations Press, 2001).

23. International Monetary Fund, *World Economic Outlook: Tensions from the Two-Speed Recovery: Unemployment, Commodities, and Capital Flows*, April 2011.

24. Paul R. Krugman, "Trade and Wages, Reconsidered," in *Brookings Papers on Economic Activity* (Washington, DC: Brookings Institution Press, 2008), pp. 103–37.

25. President's Export Council, "Letter to President Barack Obama," March 11, 2011, http://trade.gov/pec/docs/PEC_21st_Century_Trade_Letter_031111.pdf.

26. *Christian Science Monitor*, April 22, 2010. A case in point: yellow corn. In 2008, the United States held 80 percent of the Colombian market—more than one hundred million bushels. In 2010, under Colombia's trade agreement with Brazil and Argentina, tariffs on yellow corn from those countries fell to zero, versus a 15 percent tariff on U.S. corn.

27. World Bank, *Global Economic Prospects 2005*, p. xvi.

28. In their June 2010 report to G20 leaders, the director-general of the WTO, the secretary-general of the OECD, and the secretary-general of the United Nations Conference on Trade and Development (UNCTAD) wrote, "Despite the severity of the global financial crisis and its widespread impact on economies around the world, G20 governments have largely resisted pressures to erect trade and investment restrictions." For a summary, see http://www.wto.org/english/news_e/news10_e/summary_oecd_unctad_june10_e.pdf.

29. See Susan Schwab, "After Doha," *Foreign Affairs*, May/June 2011. See also the assessment of the state of the Doha negotiations by WTO director-general Pascal Lamy, http://www.wto.org.

30. See J. Bradford Jensen, "Globalization and Business Services: A Growth Opportunity," Georgetown Center for Business and Public Policy, November 2009. See also his newly released book, *Global Trade in Services: Fear, Facts and Offshoring* (Washington, DC: Peterson Institute for International Economics, 2011).

31. See United States International Trade Commission, "China: Effects of Intellectual Property Infringement and Indigenous Innovation Policies on the U.S. Economy," Investigation 332-519, May 2011.

32. See Ingo Borchert and Aaditya Mattoo, "The Crisis-Resilience of Services Trade," World Bank Policy Research Paper 4917, April 2009.

33. See Alan S. Blinder, "Offshoring: The Next Industrial Revolution?" *Foreign Affairs*, March/April 2006.

34. Jensen, "Globalization and Business Services"; see also J. Bradford Jensen and Lori G. Kletzer, "'Fear' and Offshoring: The Scope and Potential Impact of Imports and Exports of Services," Peterson Institute for International Economics, January 2008.

35. See J. Bradford Jensen, "Measuring the Impact of Trade in Services," October 2009, http://www.upjohninst.org/measurement/jensen-final.pdf.

36. European Commission, "Trade as a Driver of Prosperity," commission staff working document, 2010, p. 44.

37. See the OECD Services Trade Restrictiveness Index (STRI), http://www.oecd.org/dataoecd/15/14/46415392.pdf.

38. See Statement of Ambassador Michael Punke, Trade Negotiations Committee, WTO, March 29, 2011, http://geneva.usmission.gov/2011/03/29/ambassador-punkes-statement-on-doha.

39. See Jagdish Bhagwati, *Termites in the Trading System: How Preferential Agreements Undermine Free Trade* (Oxford: Oxford University Press, 2008).

40. See McKinsey Global Institute, "Growth and Renewal in the United States: Retooling America's Economic Engine," February 2011; see also Bruce Stokes, "Act II for American Manufacturing?" *The Next Economy*, winter 2010.

41. Martin Wolf, "How China Should Rule the World," *Financial Times*, March 23, 2011.

42. See Joseph W. Glauber, chief economist, U.S. Department of Agriculture, "Prospects for the U.S. Farm Economy in 2011," February 24, 2011.

43. All data on multinational companies come from the U.S. Department of Commerce, U.S. Bureau of Economic Analysis.

44. In 2007, 12.4 percent of these multinational firms' U.S. employees were covered by collective bargaining agreements, versus just 8.2 percent of all private-sector workers. The Bureau of Economic Analysis does not collect from U.S.-based multinationals any data on their collective bargaining.

45. Carol Corrado, Paul Lengermann, and Larry Slifman, "The Contributions of Multinational Corporations to U.S. Productivity Growth, 1977-2000," in Marshall B. Reinsdorf and Matthew J. Slaughter, eds., *International Flows of Invisibles: Trade in Services and Intangibles in the Era of Globalization* (Chicago: University of Chicago Press and NBER), pp. 331–60.

46. Matthew J. Slaughter, "Small and Big Business: Working Together for America's Prosperity," Business Roundtable research report, Washington, DC, September 2010.

47. All data are from the U.S. Department of Commerce, Bureau of Economic Analysis. For U.S.-based multinationals, years ending in 4 and 9 have traditionally been benchmark-survey years in which BEA surveys of these firms are much more extensive. For the U.S. affiliates of foreign-based multinationals, the similar benchmark-survey years have traditionally ended in 2 and 7. Data for benchmark-survey years are somewhat more reliable than data for intervening annual-survey years, where data are imputed.

48. At the time of writing, the BEA has not yet publicly released 2009 data for compensation paid by U.S. multinationals. In 2000, annual compensation in all U.S. parents averaged $49,249 and in 2008 $65,066; this nominal increase of 32.1 percent exceeded by 7.1 percent the 2000 to 2008 increase in the U.S. Consumer Price Index (CPI-U-RS) of 25 percent.

49. At the time of writing, the BEA has not yet publicly released 2009 data for U.S.-based multinationals by industry groups. Data on manufacturing employment outside U.S. parents were calculated by subtracting the BEA parent-employment data from all-manufacturing employment data as reported by the U.S. Bureau of Labor Statistics (where all-manufacturing employment was calculated to average 17.3 million in 1999 and 13.3 million in 2008).

50. For many multinationals, their U.S. and foreign operations move in tandem. This compatibility is often seen in manufacturing, in which stages of production across many countries expand or contract together. In services industries, the distribution activities of wholesale and retail trade must be performed in proximity to final customers, and affiliate expansion tends to boost many parent activities, such as logistical management and technology support. Indeed, increasing U.S. trade in services requires greater FDI in many cases. For example, consulting firms with foreign offices can create on-the-ground projects and consulting exports when specialized U.S. expertise is needed to meet particular client needs.

51. See "Moving back to America: The dwindling allure of building factories offshore," *Economist*, May 12, 2011.

52. McKinsey Global Institute, "Growth and Competitiveness in the United States: The Role of Its Multinational Companies," June 2010.

53. WTO, "Report from the Director General on Trade-Related Developments," June 14, 2010, http://www.wto.org/english/news_e/news10_e/report_tprb_june10_e.pdf.

54. The classic example in U.S.-Japan trade relations was the unsuccessful WTO challenge brought by the United States, at the behest of Kodak, to myriad restrictions in Japan designed to protect the market for Fuji, Kodak's Japanese rival. See Dick K. Nanto, "The Kodak-Fuji Filim Trade Dispute at the WTO," Congressional Research Service report 97-303-E, updated February 27, 1998.

55. Office of the United States Trade Representative, "2010 Report to Congress on China's WTO Compliance," pp. 59–61, http://www.global-trade-law.com/China-US%20%28USTR%20Report%20Jan.%202011%29.pdf.

56. See Alan William Wolff, "China in the WTO," testimony before the U.S. China Economic and Security Review Commission, Washington, DC, June 9, 2010.

57. The government of China pledged that Chinese SOEs "would make purchases and sales based solely on commercial considerations" and that "the Government of China would not influence, directly or indirectly, commercial decisions on the part of" SOEs. See "Report of the Working Party on the Accession of China," WT/ACC/CHN/49, October 1, 2001, paragraphs 46–47.

58. "2010 Report to Congress on China's WTO Compliance," p. 2.

59. The ITC surveyed more than five thousand U.S. IP-intensive firms to gather empirical data on the impact of China's IPR violations and indigenous innovation policies on the U.S. economy. The report estimates the losses to U.S. industry from IPR infringement in China totaled roughly $48 billion in 2009 and that U.S. companies spent nearly $5 billion that year to combat this infringement. United States International Trade Commission, "China: Effects of Intellectual Property Infringement and Indigenous Innovation Policies on the U.S. Economy," Investigation 332-519, May 2011.

60. Office of the United States Trade Representative, "2011 Special 301 Report," http://www.ustr.gov/webfm_send/2841.

61. See Shanker Singham, *A General Theory of Trade and Competition* (London: Cameron May, 2007), chapter 12.

62. See Office of the United States Trade Representative, "2010 National Trade Estimate Report on Foreign Trade Barriers," http://www.ustr.gov/about-us/press-office/reports-and-publications/2010.

63. In each of the previous three recessions, companies and labor unions initiated upward of eighty antidumping cases a year. Although the number of cases rose during the recent recession, it was a fraction of the number filed during the much shallower recession of 2001–2002.

64. See Daniel Ikenson, "Protection Made to Order: Domestic Industry's Capture and Reconfiguration of U.S. Antidumping Policy," Center for Trade Policy Studies, Cato Institute, December 21, 2010.

65. See "Obama Administration Strengthens Enforcement of U.S. Trade Laws in Support of President's National Export Initiative," August 26, 2010, http://www.commerce.gov/news/press-releases/2010/08/26/obama-administration-strengthens-enforcement-us-trade-laws-support-pr.

66. See Chad P. Bown, "Taking Stock of Antidumping, Safeguards and Countervailing Duties, 1990-2009," Policy Research Working Paper 5436, World Bank, Development Research Group, Trade and Integration Team, September 2010.

67. Although the decline in AD/CVD cases may partly be due to the peculiar character of the recent recession, in which trade fell sharply worldwide so that U.S. companies were not facing the surge in imports required to win relief under the statutes, the primary reason is that, in a world of global supply chains, few large U.S. companies—or big companies in any advanced developed economy—see a clear interest in raising tariffs on competitive imports. Smaller companies that do not have the same global interests have a harder time organizing themselves to mount such cases or paying the legal costs. Additionally, in more and more industries there are simply no longer any U.S. companies competing with imports.

68. The threshold for companies to win relief under WTO safeguard rules is quite high and subject to presidential discretion, which has tended to discourage companies from seeking such measures. Developing countries have been the largest users, with India leading with a total of twenty-five actions. The U.S. government needs to look at how a more effective use of safeguard measures can be made.

69. James Bacchus, *Trade and Freedom* (London: Cameron May, 2004).

70. Remarks by Jennifer Hillman, senior transatlantic fellow, German Marshall Fund of the United States and member, WTO Appellate Body, at the American University Roundtable on the Future of the WTO, September 23, 2010.

71. Among the seven cases resolved so far, four led to negotiated resolutions that were favorable to the United States but did not necessarily resolve all the issues that triggered the complaint, and the other three were decided favorably, with China agreeing to comply with the WTO rulings.

72. See Terence P. Stewart, "Evaluating China's Past and Future Role in the World Trade Organization," testimony before the U.S.-China Economic and Security Review Commission, June 9, 2010.

73. U.S.-China Economic and Security Review Commission, "Report to Congress 2010," U.S. Government Printing Office, November 2010, pp. 53–56.

74. See the recommendations in Frances G. Burwell and Annette Heuser, "Adapting the U.S.-EU Summit for a Globalized World," Atlantic Council, November 19, 2010.

75. See Greg Anderson and Christopher Sands, "Negotiating North America: The Security and Prosperity Partnership," Hudson Institute white paper, summer 2007.

76. See Leonard J. Schoppa, *Bargaining with Japan: What American Pressure Can and Cannot Do* (New York: Columbia University Press, 1997).

77. Coalition for Employment Through Exports, "Statement for the Record Before the Subcommittee on International Monetary Policy and Trade," House Committee on Financial Services, March 10, 2011.

78. "Unregulated Financing Exceeds G-7 Lending," *Washington Tariff and Trade Letter*, vol. 31, no. 21, May 23, 2011.
79. Stephen J. Ezell, "Understanding the Importance of Export Credit Financing to U.S. Competitiveness," Information Technology and Innovation Foundation, June 2011.
80. American Chamber of Commerce in Shanghai, "U.S. Export Competitiveness in China: Winning in the World's Fastest-Growing Market," September 2010, http://blog.amchamshanghai.org/wp-content/uploads/View_Point_US_Export.pdf.
81. Ibid.
82. See "White House Prepares Formal Export Strategy to Meet Demands of CEOs," *Inside U.S. Trade*, March 24, 2011.
83. Laurence Chandy and Geoffrey Gertz, "Poverty in Numbers: The Changing State of Global Poverty from 2005 to 2015," Brookings Institution, January 2011.
84. Center for Global Development, "Commitment to Development Index 2010," http://www.cgdev.org/section/initiatives/_active/cdi/.
85. IMF E-Library Data, "Direction of Trade Statistics (DOTS)," http://elibrary-data.imf.org/.
86. See Edward Gresser, "Blank Spot on the Map: How Trade Policy Is Working Against the War on Terror," Progressive Policy Institute policy report, February 2003.
87. Office of the United States Trade Representative, "Fifth Report to Congress on the Operations of the Andean Trade Preference Act as Amended," June 30, 2010, http://www.ustr.gov/sites/default/files/USTR%202010%20ATPA%20Report.pdf.
88. J. F. Hornbeck and William H. Cooper, "Trade Promotion Authority (TPA) and the Role of Congress in Trade Policy," Congressional Research Service, February 8, 2011.
89. Ibid, pp. 4–5.
90. See M. Angeles Villarreal, "The Proposed U.S.-Colombia Free Trade Agreement," Congressional Research Service report RL34470, January 26, 2011.
91. See Lael Brainard and Hal Shapiro, "Fast Track Trade Promotion Authority," Brookings Institution Policy Brief no. 91, December 2001.
92. Ibid.
93. See "The Doha Round: Setting a Deadline, Defining a Final Deal," Interim Report of the High Level Trade Experts Group, Jagdish Bhagwati and Peter Sutherland, co-chairs, January 2011.
94. See Karen H. Johnson, "Food Price Inflation: Explanation and Policy Implications," Working Paper, Council on Foreign Relations Press, July 2008.
95. From 1987 to 2006, the United States received about $2 trillion in new foreign direct investment—of which 88.8 percent was accounted for by M&A (that is, by foreign companies buying existing U.S. businesses, rather than by "green field" activity establishing new businesses).
96. World Bank Group Advisory Services, "Global Investment Promotion Benchmarking 2009: Summary Report," http://www.ifc.org/ifcext/fias.nsf/AttachmentsByTitle/GIPB2009/$FILE/GIPB2009.SummaryReport.pdf.
97. See the recommendations in Frances G. Burwell and Annette Heuser, "Adapting the U.S.-EU Summit for a Globalized World," Atlantic Council, November 19, 2010.
98. "Ex-Im Chief, Private Sector Diverge on Bank's Reauthorization Priorities," *Inside U.S. Trade*, January 14, 2011.
99. See "Maintaining America's Competitive Edge: Government Policies Affecting Semiconductor Industry R&D and Manufacturing Activity," prepared by Dewey & LeBoeuf for the Semiconductor Industry Association, March 2009.
100. See Norton Rose, LLP, and Cleantech Investor Ltd., "Cleantech Investment and Private Equity: An Industry Survey," July 2010.

101. See Center for Global Development Working Group on Trade Preference Reform, *Open Markets for the Poorest Countries: Trade Preferences That Work* (Washington, DC: Center for Global Development, 2010).

102. See Greg Mastel and Hal Shapiro, "Fast Track Forever?" *The International Economy*, summer 2006; I. M. Destler, "Renewing Fast Track Legislation," *Policy Analyses in International Economics* no. 50 (Washington, DC: Peterson Institute for International Economics, 1997).

Task Force Members

Task Force members are asked to join a consensus signifying that they endorse "the general policy thrust and judgments reached by the group, though not necessarily every finding and recommendation." They participate in the Task Force in their individual, not institutional, capacities.

Edward Alden is the Bernard L. Schwartz senior fellow at the Council on Foreign Relations, specializing in U.S. economic competitiveness. The former Washington bureau chief for the *Financial Times*, his work focuses on immigration and visa policy, and on U.S. trade and international economic policy. Alden was the project director for the Independent Task Force report *U.S. Immigration Policy*, which was chaired by former Florida governor Jeb Bush and former White House chief of staff Thomas F. McLarty III. Mr. Alden was previously the Canadian bureau chief for the *Financial Times* based in Toronto, and before that was a reporter at the *Vancouver Sun* specializing in labor and employment issues. He also worked as the managing editor of the newsletter *Inside U.S. Trade*, widely recognized as the leading source of reporting on U.S. trade policies. Alden has a bachelor's degree in political science from the University of British Columbia. He holds a master's degree in international relations from the University of California, Berkeley, and pursued doctoral studies before returning to a journalism career.

Nancy Birdsall is the Center for Global Development's founding president. She was executive vice president of the Inter-American Development Bank, the largest of the regional development banks, where she oversaw a $30 billion public and private loan portfolio. Before that she worked for fourteen years in research, policy, and management positions at the World Bank, including as director of the Policy Research department. Prior to launching the center, she served for three years as senior associate and director of the Economic Reform Project at the

Carnegie Endowment for International Peace, where her work focused on globalization, inequality, and the reform of the international financial institutions. She is the author, coauthor, or editor of more than a dozen books and over one hundred articles in scholarly journals and monographs. Shorter pieces of her writing have appeared in dozens of U.S. and Latin American newspapers and periodicals. Birdsall received her MA from the Johns Hopkins School of Advanced International Studies and her PhD from Yale University.

James J. Blanchard is co-chair of government affairs at the global law firm of DLA Piper LLP (U.S.). Previously, he served as U.S. ambassador to Canada from 1993 to 1996, after having served two terms as governor of Michigan and four terms as a member of the U.S. Congress. In 1992, he chaired President Bill Clinton's successful campaign in Michigan. Blanchard is also former chairman of the Democratic Governors Association and the National Democratic Platform Committee, as well as a former member of the National Governors Association's executive committee. His eight years as Michigan's chief executive were notable for his success in turning around Michigan's finances, working with the private sector to attract business investment and trade from around the world. Prior to his election to Congress, he was assistant attorney general of Michigan. In 2010, he was named co-chair of the Canada-United States Law Institute, a forum where the two countries' governments, business communities, legal professionals, academics, nongovernmental organizations, and media address issues confronting U.S.-Canada relations. Blanchard served on Senator Hillary Clinton's national finance committee. He serves on the board of directors of several corporations and, in February 2005, co-chaired the American Assembly project on U.S.-Canada relations, hosted and sponsored by Columbia University.

Andrew H. Card is acting dean of the Bush School of Government and Public Service at Texas A&M University. He was appointed chief of staff in the presidential administration of former Texas governor George W. Bush. Card served as the eleventh U.S. secretary of transportation under President George H.W. Bush. He also served in the George H.W. Bush administration as assistant to the president and deputy chief of staff. Card served under President Ronald Reagan as special assistant to the president for intergovernmental affairs and as deputy assistant to the president and director of intergovernmental affairs. He was president and CEO of the American Automobile Manufacturers Association (AAMA), the trade association. He served in the Massachusetts House of Representatives from 1975 to 1983. Currently, Card is also senior counselor at the global public relations firm Fleischman-Hillard, serving on the international advisory board. He serves on the board of directors at Union Pacific Corporation. He also serves on the U.S. Chamber of Commerce advisory board, an advisory board for Alexander Proudfoot, and some privately held corporate and nonprofit boards. Card graduated from the University of South Carolina with a Bachelor of Science degree. He attended the United States Merchant Marine Academy and the John F. Kennedy School of Government at Harvard University.

Thomas A. Daschle graduated from South Dakota State University in 1969. Upon graduation, he entered the U.S. Air Force, where he served as an intelligence officer in the Strategic Air Command until mid-1972. Following completion of his military service, Daschle served on the staff of Senator James Abourezk. In 1978, he was elected to the U.S. House of Representatives, where he served for eight years. In 1986, he was elected to the U.S. Senate and eight years later became its Democratic leader. Today, Daschle is a senior policy adviser to the law firm of DLA Piper. In 2007, he collaborated to create the Bipartisan Policy Center, an organization dedicated to finding common ground on some of the pressing public policy challenges. Daschle serves on the board of the Center for American Progress, acts as the vice chair of the National Democratic Institute, and is a member of the Council on Foreign Relations. He is a member of the Lyndon Baines Johnson Foundation board of trustees, the GE Healthymagination advisory board; the National Integrated Foodsystem advisory board; and the Committee on Collaborative Initiatives at the Massachusetts Institute of Technology. In addition, Daschle's board memberships include the Blum Foundation, the Energy Future Coalition, the Committee to Modernize Voter Registration, the U.S. Global Leadership Coalition advisory council, and the Advisory Committee on the Trust for National Mall.

I. M. (Mac) Destler is the Saul I. Stern professor of civic engagement at the Maryland School of Public Policy. His scholarly work centers on the politics and processes of U.S. foreign policymaking. He is coauthor, with Ivo H. Daalder, of *In the Shadow of the Oval Office*, which analyzes the role of the president's national security adviser from the Kennedy through George W. Bush administrations. His *American Trade Politics* won the Gladys M. Kammerer Award from the American Political Science Association for the best book on U.S. national policy. Destler is also a fellow at the Peterson Institute for International Economics (IIE), where he conducts research on the political economy of trade policymaking. He has consulted on government organization for economic and foreign policymaking at the Executive Office of the President and the Department of State and has held senior research positions at IIE, the Carnegie Endowment for International Peace, and the Brookings Institution. He is the recipient of the University of Maryland's Distinguished International Service Award for 1998. Destler teaches trade policy, American foreign policymaking, and political institutions, and directs the Master of Public Policy program in international security and economic policy.

Harold E. Ford Jr. is managing director and senior client relationship manager at Morgan Stanley. Previously, he was executive vice chairman of global banking and wealth management at Bank of America. Ford served ten years in the U.S. Congress. Elected at twenty-six, he served on the House Financial Services and Budget committees. Described by President Bill Clinton as "the walking, living embodiment of where America ought to go in the twenty-first century," Ford also chairs the Democratic Leadership Council and is a distinguished practitioner in residence at the Wagner School of Public Service at NYU. During Ford's five terms in Congress, he was an active member of the House Blue Dog coalition, where he worked passionately to balance the budget and promote free enterprise. Ford serves as an overseer for the International Rescue Committee, is a member of the Pentagon's Transformation Advisory Group and the Council on Foreign Relations, and serves on the boards of directors of America's Promise and the Posse Foundation. Ford is a graduate of the University of Pennsylvania and the University of Michigan Law School.

Leo W. Gerard* serves as the international president of the United Steelworkers (USW), a position he was elected to in 2001. As president of the USW, Gerard was instrumental in the formation of the Industrial Union Council of the American Federation of Labor and Congress

---

*Gerard participated as a member of the Task Force but did not endorse the general thrust of the final report.

of Industrial Organizations (AFL-CIO) and in February 2003 was appointed to serve on the AFL-CIO's executive committee and executive council. He is also a board member of the AFL-CIO Transportation Trades department and chairs the AFL-CIO public policy committee. Prior to becoming president of the USW, Gerard served as the union's international secretary-treasurer, as national director of Canada, and as director of District 6 in Ontario. He was also appointed a USW staff representative. In addition, Gerard serves on the U.S. National Commission on Energy Policy, is a founding board member of the Apollo Alliance, and is co-chairman of the board of the Blue Green Alliance.

Daniel R. Glickman is currently the executive director of the Aspen Institute Congressional Program and a senior fellow at the Bipartisan Policy Center in Washington, DC. Glickman served as chairman of the Motion Picture Association of America, Inc. (MPAA), from 2004 until 2010. Glickman served as the U.S. secretary of agriculture from March 1995 until January 2001 and served for eighteen years in the U.S. House of Representatives representing the 4th Congressional District of Kansas. Glickman serves as vice chair of the board of World Food Program USA and is a board member of Communities in Schools, the Chicago Mercantile Exchange, Oxfam America, Food Research and Action Center, National 4-H Council, and the Center for U.S. Global Engagement, where he is chair of the U.S. Global Leadership Coalition. Glickman co-chairs an initiative called AGree, which looks at long-term domestic and international implications of food and agricultural policy. He also chairs an initiative at the Institute of Medicine on accelerating progress on childhood obesity. He is a member of the Council on Foreign Relations and serves as co-chair of the Chicago Council on Global Affairs global agriculture development initiative, and he coauthored "Farm Futures" in *Foreign Affairs* (May/June 2009).

Robert E. Litan is the vice president for research and policy at the Kauffman Foundation in Kansas City and a senior fellow in economic studies at the Brookings Institution. He has served in several government positions, including as associate director of the Office of Management and Budget, deputy assistant attorney general of the Department of Justice's antitrust division, and staff economist at the Council of Economic Advisers. He has also consulted for numerous public and private sector organizations, including the Department of the Treasury and the World Bank. During his career, Litan has authored or coauthored more than twenty-five books, edited another fourteen, and authored or coauthored more than two hundred articles in journals, magazines, and newspapers on government policies affecting financial institutions, regulatory and legal issues, international trade, and the economy in general. His most recent book is *Good Capitalism, Bad Capitalism, and the Economics of Growth and Prosperity.*

Trent Lott serves as senior counsel at Patton Boggs LLP. Previously, he represented the people of Mississippi in Congress for thirty-five years and is one of a handful of officials to have held elected leadership positions in both the House of Representatives and Senate. During his sixteen years in the House and nineteen years in the Senate, he worked closely with seven presidential administrations and was regarded as a savvy coalition builder and dealmaker. Lott joined the House in 1973, representing Mississippi's Fifth Congressional District. From 1981 to 1989, he served as House minority whip, forging the bipartisan alliance that enacted Ronald Reagan's economic recovery program and national security initiatives. He also founded the House's first modern whip organization with a focus on regular member-to-member contacts and extensive outreach to sympathetic Democrats to secure passage of major legislation. In 1988, Lott was elected to the Senate. In 2006, he was elected Senate Republican whip, giving him the distinction of being the only person to hold that position in both the House and Senate. Before joining Patton Boggs, Lott and fellow former senator John Breaux founded the Breaux-Lott Leadership Group.

Kevin G. Nealer is a principal and partner in the Scowcroft Group, an international business advisory firm. In this capacity, Nealer provides risk analysis and direct investment support to the group's multinational clients. Nealer has lead responsibility for the firm's support for the investment community, providing analysis to leading currency and equity/debt traders. In addition, he assists industrial and financial clients in project planning and implementing investment and workout strategies. Previously, Nealer served on the professional staff of the Senate Democratic Policy Committee, where he worked on trade and international economic policy and was a Foreign Service officer with the State Department. Nealer has served as a lecturer, program moderator, and adjunct professor of trade law and policy at the Georgetown University McDonough School of Business and was a Fulbright professor in

China. Nealer received his undergraduate degree from the University of Michigan and his law degree from Case Western Reserve University School of Law. Following his confirmation by the U.S. Senate, Nealer was sworn in as a member of the board of directors of the Overseas Private Investment Corporation, the development finance agency of the U.S. government, where he serves on the audit committee.

James W. Owens served as chairman and CEO of Caterpillar Inc. in Peoria, Illinois, from 2004 through June 2010. Owens was named chairman and CEO of Caterpillar in 2004 after spending his entire career at the company. In his first five years, 2004 to 2008, Caterpillar's revenue grew from $22.8 billion to $51.3 billion, setting sales and profit records every year. Owens is currently a director of Alcoa Inc. in Pittsburgh, Pennsylvania; IBM Corporation in Armonk, New York; and Morgan Stanley in New York City. He also serves as a senior adviser to Kohlberg Kravis Roberts & Co. in New York. Owens is chairman of the Executive Committee for the Peterson Institute for International Economics in Washington, DC, and a member of the Board of Directors of the Council on Foreign Relations in New York. He serves on the executive committee of the Business Council and was a member of President Obama's Economic Recovery Advisory Board from 2009 to 2010. He is also a member of the board of trustees for North Carolina State University in Raleigh, North Carolina. Owens is a native of Elizabeth City, North Carolina, and graduated from North Carolina State University in 1973 with a PhD in economics.

William F. Owens is a senior fellow of the University of Denver's Institute for Public Policy Studies and a special guest instructor in the undergraduate and graduate programs. Owens, who served two terms as governor of Colorado, was called "the best governor in America" by *National Review* magazine and has been praised by the Cato Institute and the *Wall Street Journal* for his pro-growth economic policies. Owens presently serves on the boards of four New York Stock Exchange firms, advises two private equity firms, and is on the board of Russia's second-largest railroad. Prior to his service as governor, Owens served as state treasurer and was elected to both the Colorado House and Senate. He has been a regular speaker and panelist at the World Economic Forum in Davos, Switzerland, and a guest lecturer at Moscow State University; the University of Kazan; New Russian University (Moscow); British/

American University in Alma Aty, Kazakhstan; and the University
of Dublin. Owens earned a Master of Public Affairs degree from the
Lyndon B. Johnson School of Public Affairs at the University of Texas
at Austin.

Pamela S. Passman is corporate vice president and deputy general
counsel for Microsoft and has led its Global Corporate and Regulatory Affairs function since 2002. Her responsibilities have included
providing regulatory counsel to business groups and developing corporate positions on public policy issues, such as intellectual property
rights, privacy, Internet security, international trade, and telecommunications; strengthening government and industry relations; developing partnerships with governments, international organizations,
nonprofits and industry; and overseeing Microsoft's philanthropic
investments. From 1996 to 2002, Passman served in Tokyo as associate general counsel, responsible for Microsoft's Law and Corporate
Affairs groups in Japan, South Korea, Taiwan, and the People's Republic of China, including Hong Kong. Prior to joining Microsoft, Passman
was with Covington & Burling in Washington, DC. She also practiced
in Japan with Nagashima & Ohno and served as special counsel to the
Office of Political and Economic Research, Itochu Corporation. Passman is chair of the Board of Information Technology Industry Council and serves on the boards of Business for Social Responsibility, the
National Bureau of Asian Research, and Kids in Need of Defense.
She is a graduate of Lafayette College and the University of Virginia
School of Law. She was also a recipient of a Watson Foundation grant
for research in Japan.

Matthew J. Slaughter is associate dean and Signal Companies' professor
of management at the Tuck School of Business at Dartmouth College. He
is also currently an adjunct senior fellow at the Council on Foreign Relations; a research associate at the National Bureau of Economic Research;
a member of the academic advisory board of the International Tax Policy
Forum; an academic adviser to both the Deloitte Center on Cross-
Border Investment and the Organization for International Investment;
and a member of the U.S. State Department's Advisory Committee on
International Economic Policy. Slaughter served as a member on the
Council of Economic Advisers in the Executive Office of the President.
In this Senate-confirmed position, he held the international portfolio,

advising the president, the cabinet, and others on issues including international trade and investment, energy, and the competitiveness of the U.S. economy. He has also been affiliated with the Federal Reserve Board, the International Monetary Fund, the World Bank, the National Academy of Sciences, the McKinsey Global Institute, the Institute for International Economics, and the Department of Labor. Slaughter received his bachelor's degree from the University of Notre Dame and his doctorate from the Massachusetts Institute of Technology.

Andrew L. Stern is the former president of the 2.2 million member Service Employees International Union (SEIU), the largest union of health-care, hospital, nursing home, home-care, janitorial, security, child-care, food service, and state workers, and the fastest-growing union in North America. SEIU was widely credited for creating the most effective grassroots political organization and raising the country's largest political action fund that helped elect President Barack Obama. Called a "courageous, visionary leader who charted a bold new course for American unionism," the union was recognized as the most engaged and influential advocate of health-care reform, helping secure the historic passage of the 2010 Health Care Reform Act. Stern continues that work as a fellow at the Georgetown University Public Policy Institute and as director of AmericaWorks, a project of the Tides Foundation. He was named in 2010 as a presidential appointee to the National Commission on Fiscal Responsibility and Reform. Stern began working as a social service worker and member of SEIU Local 668 in 1973. He served as organizing director for SEIU before his landmark election as its youngest president in 1996. Stern is a graduate of the University of Pennsylvania.

William M. Thomas was a member of the U.S. House of Representatives for twenty-eight years and has spent his career strengthening health-care legislation, reducing tax burdens, advocating free and open trade, and protecting workers' pensions. Thomas continues his examination of substantial economic issues in search of coalition-building solutions through his work as a visiting fellow at the American Enterprise Institute. During his six years as chairman of the House Ways and Means Committee, Thomas helped the president attain Trade Promotion Authority (TPA) and guided seven free trade agreements through Congress. After nearly a decade with few comprehensive free trade agreements, Thomas led the charge in Congress to reauthorize TPA and empower the president with the necessary negotiating ability to open new markets to U.S. exports and create more American jobs. Thomas also was responsible for reforming Medicare legislation, nearly $2 trillion in tax relief, and reforms to the U.S. pension system. He also led efforts to reduce the tax burden on small businesses, manufacturers, and other job creators through a new tax deduction for domestic manufacturing activities; enhanced Section 179 expensing for small businesses; and introduced international tax reforms to make U.S.-based companies that operate abroad more competitive.

Laura D'Andrea Tyson is the S. K. and Angela Chan professor of global management at the University of California, Berkeley, Haas School of Business. She was previously dean of the London Business School and the Haas School of Business. Tyson is also a member of President Obama's Council on Jobs and Competitiveness. She served in the Clinton administration and was the chair of the Council of Economic Advisers and the National Economic Council. Tyson is a senior adviser at the McKinsey Global Institute, Credit Suisse Research Institute, and the Rock Creek Group; a senior fellow at the Center for American Progress; and a member of the MIT Corporation and National Academies Board on Science, Technology, and Economic Policy. Tyson is on the advisory council of the Brookings Institution Hamilton Project and is an advisory board member of Newman's Own, Generation Investment Management, and H&Q Asia Pacific. She is also a special adviser to the Berkeley Research Group and a member of the Committee on Capital Markets Regulation and the National Academies Committee on Research Universities. Tyson serves on the boards of directors of Eastman Kodak Company, Morgan Stanley, AT&T, Silver Spring Networks, CB Richard Ellis, the Peter G. Peterson Institute of International Economics, New America Foundation, and the Committee for a Responsible Federal Budget.

John K. Veroneau is a partner at Covington and Burling LLP and co-chair of the international trade and finance practice group. Veroneau served as deputy U.S. trade representative (USTR). He previously served as the USTR's general counsel, responsible for U.S. trade law and litigation activities. In these capacities, he worked on a wide range of matters, including negotiating trade and investment agreements, initiating and defending World Trade Organization disputes, executing

U.S. trade laws (such as Section 421 China safeguards and Section 337 infringement cases), and assisting U.S. companies to overcome foreign regulatory barriers. As deputy USTR, Veroneau made official visits to more than thirty countries and represented the USTR on various government boards, including the Committee on Foreign Investment in the United States, Export-Import Bank, Overseas Private Investment Corporation, and Millennium Challenge Corporation. He was also confirmed by the U.S. Senate to serve as an assistant secretary of defense in President Bill Clinton's administration. He has extensive legislative branch experience, having served as legislative director to Senator Bill Cohen (R-ME) and Majority Leader Bill Frist (R-TN) and as chief of staff to Senator Susan Collins (R-ME).

Carmencita N. Whonder is a policy director in the Washington, DC, office of Brownstein Hyatt Farber Schreck, LLP, where she is a member of the government relations department. She provides strategic public policy advice to clients primarily in the financial services and housing sectors before the U.S. Congress and executive branch agencies. Prior to joining Brownstein, Whonder served as the staff director for the Senate Subcommittee on Housing, Transportation, and Community Development and as the principal adviser on the Senate Banking, Housing, and Urban Affairs Committee to U.S. Senator Charles E. Schumer (D-NY). During the 109th Congress she held the position of minority staff director for the Senate Subcommittee on Economic Policy. For four years, Whonder was responsible for issues including banking, financial institutions, securities and commodities markets, economic and monetary policy, the Committee on Foreign Investment in the United States, insurance, consumer protection, housing and community development, and trade. She previously worked as a leadership education counselor for Gates Millennium Scholars Program/UNCF. In 2000, Whonder worked in Geneva, Switzerland, at the World Intellectual Property Organization, a United Nations specialized agency, focusing on e-commerce and trade issues. Whonder holds a bachelor's degree from Howard University and a master's degree from the Johns Hopkins University School of Advanced International Studies.

Alan Wm. Wolff co-chairs the International Trade Practice of Dewey & LeBoeuf. He is chairman of the National Foreign Trade Council, the comparative innovation committee of the Science, Technology, and

Economic Policy Board of the National Academies, and of the board of the Institute for Trade and Commercial Diplomacy, and is a member of the advisory committee of the Peterson Institute for International Economics and of the board of the U.S.-China Legal Cooperation Fund. From 2010 to June 2011, he was distinguished research professor at the Monterey Institute of International Studies, a graduate school of Middlebury College. Wolff served as deputy special representative for trade negotiations in the Carter administration and was general counsel of that office in the Ford administration, after holding senior positions in the Treasury Department. He has served on a number of government advisory committees, including the President's Advisory Committee on Negotiations under Carter, the Services Policy Advisory Committee under Reagan, and the State Department's Advisory Committee on International Economic Policy under Bush and Obama. Wolff has written extensively and testified on trade policy issues. He is a national associate of the National Academies and is a member of the bar in New York, Massachusetts, and the District of Columbia. He is a graduate of Columbia Law School and Harvard College.

Independent Task Force Reports

Published by the Council on Foreign Relations

Global Brazil and U.S.-Brazil Relations
Samuel W. Bodman and James D. Wolfensohn, Chairs; Julia E. Sweig, Project Director
Independent Task Force Report No. 66 (2011)

U.S. Strategy for Pakistan and Afghanistan
Richard L. Armitage and Samuel R. Berger, Chairs; Daniel S. Markey, Project Director
Independent Task Force Report No. 65 (2010)

U.S. Policy Toward the Korean Peninsula
Charles L. Pritchard and John H. Tilelli Jr., Chairs; Scott A. Snyder, Project Director
Independent Task Force Report No. 64 (2010)

U.S. Immigration Policy
Jeb Bush and Thomas F. McLarty III, Chairs; Edward Alden, Project Director
Independent Task Force Report No. 63 (2009)

U.S. Nuclear Weapons Policy
William J. Perry and Brent Scowcroft, Chairs; Charles D. Ferguson, Project Director
Independent Task Force Report No. 62 (2009)

Confronting Climate Change: A Strategy for U.S. Foreign Policy
George E. Pataki and Thomas J. Vilsack, Chairs; Michael A. Levi, Project Director
Independent Task Force Report No. 61 (2008)

U.S.-Latin America Relations: A New Direction for a New Reality
Charlene Barshefsky and James T. Hill, Chairs; Shannon O'Neil, Project Director
Independent Task Force Report No. 60 (2008)

U.S.-China Relations: An Affirmative Agenda, A Responsible Course
Carla A. Hills and Dennis C. Blair, Chairs; Frank Sampson Jannuzi, Project Director
Independent Task Force Report No. 59 (2007)

National Security Consequences of U.S. Oil Dependency
John Deutch and James R. Schlesinger, Chairs; David G. Victor, Project Director
Independent Task Force Report No. 58 (2006)

Russia's Wrong Direction: What the United States Can and Should Do
John Edwards and Jack Kemp, Chairs; Stephen Sestanovich, Project Director
Independent Task Force Report No. 57 (2006)

More than Humanitarianism: A Strategic U.S. Approach Toward Africa
Anthony Lake and Christine Todd Whitman, Chairs; Princeton N. Lyman and J. Stephen Morrison, Project Directors
Independent Task Force Report No. 56 (2006)

In the Wake of War: Improving Post-Conflict Capabilities
Samuel R. Berger and Brent Scowcroft, Chairs; William L. Nash, Project Director; Mona K. Sutphen, Deputy Director
Independent Task Force Report No. 55 (2005)

In Support of Arab Democracy: Why and How
Madeleine K. Albright and Vin Weber, Chairs; Steven A. Cook, Project Director
Independent Task Force Report No. 54 (2005)

Building a North American Community
John P. Manley, Pedro Aspe, and William F. Weld, Chairs; Thomas d'Aquino, Andrés Rozental, and Robert Pastor, Vice Chairs; Chappell H. Lawson, Project Director
Independent Task Force Report No. 53 (2005)

Iran: Time for a New Approach
Zbigniew Brzezinski and Robert M. Gates, Chairs; Suzanne Maloney, Project Director
Independent Task Force Report No. 52 (2004)

An Update on the Global Campaign Against Terrorist Financing
Maurice R. Greenberg, Chair; William F. Wechsler and Lee S. Wolosky, Project Directors
Independent Task Force Report No. 40B (Web-only release, 2004)

Renewing the Atlantic Partnership
Henry A. Kissinger and Lawrence H. Summers, Chairs; Charles A. Kupchan, Project Director
Independent Task Force Report No. 51 (2004)

Iraq: One Year After
Thomas R. Pickering and James R. Schlesinger, Chairs; Eric P. Schwartz, Project Consultant
Independent Task Force Report No. 43C (Web-only release, 2004)

Nonlethal Weapons and Capabilities
Paul X. Kelley and Graham Allison, Chairs; Richard L. Garwin, Project Director
Independent Task Force Report No. 50 (2004)

New Priorities in South Asia: U.S. Policy Toward India, Pakistan, and Afghanistan (Chairmen's Report)
Marshall Bouton, Nicholas Platt, and Frank G. Wisner, Chairs; Dennis Kux and Mahnaz Ispahani, Project Directors
Independent Task Force Report No. 49 (2003)
Cosponsored with the Asia Society

Finding America's Voice: A Strategy for Reinvigorating U.S. Public Diplomacy
Peter G. Peterson, Chair; Kathy Bloomgarden, Henry Grunwald, David E. Morey, and Shibley Telhami, Working Committee Chairs; Jennifer Sieg, Project Director; Sharon Herbstman, Project Coordinator
Independent Task Force Report No. 48 (2003)

Emergency Responders: Drastically Underfunded, Dangerously Unprepared
Warren B. Rudman, Chair; Richard A. Clarke, Senior Adviser; Jamie F. Metzl,
Project Director
Independent Task Force Report No. 47 (2003)

Iraq: The Day After (Chairs' Update)
Thomas R. Pickering and James R. Schlesinger, Chairs; Eric P. Schwartz, Project Director
Independent Task Force Report No. 43B (Web-only release, 2003)

Burma: Time for Change
Mathea Falco, Chair
Independent Task Force Report No. 46 (2003)

Afghanistan: Are We Losing the Peace?
Marshall Bouton, Nicholas Platt, and Frank G. Wisner, Chairs; Dennis Kux and Mahnaz
Ispahani, Project Directors
Chairman's Report of an Independent Task Force (2003)
Cosponsored with the Asia Society

Meeting the North Korean Nuclear Challenge
Morton I. Abramowitz and James T. Laney, Chairs; Eric Heginbotham, Project Director
Independent Task Force Report No. 45 (2003)

Chinese Military Power
Harold Brown, Chair; Joseph W. Prueher, Vice Chair; Adam Segal, Project Director
Independent Task Force Report No. 44 (2003)

Iraq: The Day After
Thomas R. Pickering and James R. Schlesinger, Chairs; Eric P. Schwartz, Project Director
Independent Task Force Report No. 43 (2003)

Threats to Democracy: Prevention and Response
Madeleine K. Albright and Bronislaw Geremek, Chairs; Morton H. Halperin, Director;
Elizabeth Frawley Bagley, Associate Director
Independent Task Force Report No. 42 (2002)

America—Still Unprepared, Still in Danger
Gary Hart and Warren B. Rudman, Chairs; Stephen E. Flynn, Project Director
Independent Task Force Report No. 41 (2002)

Terrorist Financing
Maurice R. Greenberg, Chair; William F. Wechsler and Lee S. Wolosky, Project Directors
Independent Task Force Report No. 40 (2002)

Enhancing U.S. Leadership at the United Nations
David Dreier and Lee H. Hamilton, Chairs; Lee Feinstein and Adrian Karatnycky, Project
Directors
Independent Task Force Report No. 39 (2002)
Cosponsored with Freedom House

Improving the U.S. Public Diplomacy Campaign in the War Against Terrorism
Carla A. Hills and Richard C. Holbrooke, Chairs; Charles G. Boyd, Project Director
Independent Task Force Report No. 38 (Web-only release, 2001)

Building Support for More Open Trade
Kenneth M. Duberstein and Robert E. Rubin, Chairs; Timothy F. Geithner, Project Director;
Daniel R. Lucich, Deputy Project Director
Independent Task Force Report No. 37 (2001)

Beginning the Journey: China, the United States, and the WTO
Robert D. Hormats, Chair; Elizabeth Economy and Kevin Nealer, Project Directors
Independent Task Force Report No. 36 (2001)

Strategic Energy Policy Update
Edward L. Morse, Chair; Amy Myers Jaffe, Project Director
Independent Task Force Report No. 33B (2001)
Cosponsored with the James A. Baker III Institute for Public Policy of Rice University

Testing North Korea: The Next Stage in U.S. and ROK Policy
Morton I. Abramowitz and James T. Laney, Chairs; Robert A. Manning, Project Director
Independent Task Force Report No. 35 (2001)

The United States and Southeast Asia: A Policy Agenda for the New Administration
J. Robert Kerrey, Chair; Robert A. Manning, Project Director
Independent Task Force Report No. 34 (2001)

Strategic Energy Policy: Challenges for the 21st Century
Edward L. Morse, Chair; Amy Myers Jaffe, Project Director
Independent Task Force Report No. 33 (2001)
Cosponsored with the James A. Baker III Institute for Public Policy of Rice University

A Letter to the President and a Memorandum on U.S. Policy Toward Brazil
Stephen Robert, Chair; Kenneth Maxwell, Project Director
Independent Task Force Report No. 32 (2001)

State Department Reform
Frank C. Carlucci, Chair; Ian J. Brzezinski, Project Coordinator
Independent Task Force Report No. 31 (2001)
Cosponsored with the Center for Strategic and International Studies

U.S.-Cuban Relations in the 21st Century: A Follow-on Report
Bernard W. Aronson and William D. Rogers, Chairs; Julia Sweig and Walter Mead, Project
Directors
Independent Task Force Report No. 30 (2000)

Toward Greater Peace and Security in Colombia: Forging a Constructive U.S. Policy
Bob Graham and Brent Scowcroft, Chairs; Michael Shifter, Project Director
Independent Task Force Report No. 29 (2000)
Cosponsored with the Inter-American Dialogue

Future Directions for U.S. Economic Policy Toward Japan
Laura D'Andrea Tyson, Chair; M. Diana Helweg Newton, Project Director
Independent Task Force Report No. 28 (2000)

First Steps Toward a Constructive U.S. Policy in Colombia
Bob Graham and Brent Scowcroft, Chairs; Michael Shifter, Project Director
Interim Report (2000)
Cosponsored with the Inter-American Dialogue

Promoting Sustainable Economies in the Balkans
Steven Rattner, Chair; Michael B.G. Froman, Project Director
Independent Task Force Report No. 27 (2000)

Non-Lethal Technologies: Progress and Prospects
Richard L. Garwin, Chair; W. Montague Winfield, Project Director
Independent Task Force Report No. 26 (1999)

Safeguarding Prosperity in a Global Financial System:
The Future International Financial Architecture
Carla A. Hills and Peter G. Peterson, Chairs; Morris Goldstein, Project Director
Independent Task Force Report No. 25 (1999)
Cosponsored with the International Institute for Economics

U.S. Policy Toward North Korea: Next Steps
Morton I. Abramowitz and James T. Laney, Chairs; Michael J. Green, Project Director
Independent Task Force Report No. 24 (1999)

Reconstructing the Balkans
Morton I. Abramowitz and Albert Fishlow, Chairs; Charles A. Kupchan, Project Director
Independent Task Force Report No. 23 (Web-only release, 1999)

Strengthening Palestinian Public Institutions
Michel Rocard, Chair; Henry Siegman, Project Director; Yezid Sayigh and Khalil Shikaki,
Principal Authors
Independent Task Force Report No. 22 (1999)

U.S. Policy Toward Northeastern Europe
Zbigniew Brzezinski, Chair; F. Stephen Larrabee, Project Director
Independent Task Force Report No. 21 (1999)

The Future of Transatlantic Relations
Robert D. Blackwill, Chair and Project Director
Independent Task Force Report No. 20 (1999)

U.S.-Cuban Relations in the 21st Century
Bernard W. Aronson and William D. Rogers, Chairs; Walter Russell Mead, Project Director
Independent Task Force Report No. 19 (1999)

After the Tests: U.S. Policy Toward India and Pakistan
Richard N. Haass and Morton H. Halperin, Chairs
Independent Task Force Report No. 18 (1998)
Cosponsored with the Brookings Institution

Managing Change on the Korean Peninsula
Morton I. Abramowitz and James T. Laney, Chairs; Michael J. Green, Project Director
Independent Task Force Report No. 17 (1998)

Promoting U.S. Economic Relations with Africa
Peggy Dulany and Frank Savage, Chairs; Salih Booker, Project Director
Independent Task Force Report No. 16 (1998)

U.S. Middle East Policy and the Peace Process
Henry Siegman, Project Coordinator
Independent Task Force Report No. 15 (1997)

Differentiated Containment: U.S. Policy Toward Iran and Iraq
Zbigniew Brzezinski and Brent Scowcroft, Chairs; Richard W. Murphy, Project Director
Independent Task Force Report No. 14 (1997)

Russia, Its Neighbors, and an Enlarging NATO
Richard G. Lugar, Chair; Victoria Nuland, Project Director
Independent Task Force Report No. 13 (1997)

Rethinking International Drug Control: New Directions for U.S. Policy
Mathea Falco, Chair
Independent Task Force Report No. 12 (1997)

Financing America's Leadership: Protecting American Interests and Promoting American Values
Mickey Edwards and Stephen J. Solarz, Chairs; Morton H. Halperin, Lawrence J. Korb,
and Richard M. Moose, Project Directors
Independent Task Force Report No. 11 (1997)
Cosponsored with the Brookings Institution

A New U.S. Policy Toward India and Pakistan
Richard N. Haass, Chair; Gideon Rose, Project Director
Independent Task Force Report No. 10 (1997)

Arms Control and the U.S.-Russian Relationship
Robert D. Blackwill, Chair and Author; Keith W. Dayton, Project Director
Independent Task Force Report No. 9 (1996)
Cosponsored with the Nixon Center for Peace and Freedom

American National Interest and the United Nations
George Soros, Chair
Independent Task Force Report No. 8 (1996)

Making Intelligence Smarter: The Future of U.S. Intelligence
Maurice R. Greenberg, Chair; Richard N. Haass, Project Director
Independent Task Force Report No. 7 (1996)

Lessons of the Mexican Peso Crisis
John C. Whitehead, Chair; Marie-Josée Kravis, Project Director
Independent Task Force Report No. 6 (1996)

Managing the Taiwan Issue: Key Is Better U.S. Relations with China
Stephen Friedman, Chair; Elizabeth Economy, Project Director
Independent Task Force Report No. 5 (1995)

Non-Lethal Technologies: Military Options and Implications
Malcolm H. Wiener, Chair
Independent Task Force Report No. 4 (1995)

Should NATO Expand?
Harold Brown, Chair; Charles A. Kupchan, Project Director
Independent Task Force Report No. 3 (1995)

Success or Sellout? The U.S.-North Korean Nuclear Accord
Kyung Won Kim and Nicholas Platt, Chairs; Richard N. Haass, Project Director
Independent Task Force Report No. 2 (1995)
Cosponsored with the Seoul Forum for International Affairs

Nuclear Proliferation: Confronting the New Challenges
Stephen J. Hadley, Chair; Mitchell B. Reiss, Project Director
Independent Task Force Report No. 1 (1995)

To purchase a printed copy, call the Brookings Institution Press: 800.537.5487.
Note: Task Force reports are available for download from CFR's website, www.cfr.org.
For more information, email publications@cfr.org.